BM EDUCATIO  KT-510-828

JAPAN
FROM SHOGUN TO SUPERSTATE

STUART FEWSTER
TONY GORTON

WITH A FOREWORD BY GORDON DANIELS
General Editor & Academic Adviser

Paul Norbury Publications
Woodchurch, Ashford, Kent

Paul Norbury Publications
Woodchurch, Ashford, Kent TN26 3TW, England

© Stuart Fewster & Tony Gorton 1987
First published by Paul Norbury Publications 1988

ISBN 0-904404-59-5 (Paper)
ISBN 0-904404-67-6 (Cloth)

All rights reserved. No part of this publication may be reproduced or
transmitted in any form or by any means without permission

The publishers wish to express their sincere thanks to:
The Japan Foundation (Kokusai Koryu Kikin)
and
The Great Britain-Sasakawa Foundation
for their kind assistance and support in the making of this book.

*The publishers are also indebted to Mr Vivien Thomas (Senior Adviser, Humanities,
West Glamorgan County Council) for his invaluable assistance in the planning of this project.*

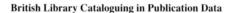

British Library Cataloguing in Publication Data

Fewster, Stuart
    Japan: from shogun to superstate.
    1. Japan—History—Restoration, 1853-1870
    2. Japan—History—1868-
    I. Title II. Gorton, Tony
    952.03 DS881.3

    ISBN 0-904404-67-6
    ISBN 0-904404-59-5 Pbk

WITHDRAWN
BM8J
(FEW) 12389

STUART FEWSTER is Head of Humanities, St Stephen-in-Brannel School, Cornwall
TONY GORTON is Teacher of Asian History, Atlantic College, South Glamorgan
GORDON DANIELS is Senior Lecturer in Modern Japanese History, University of Sheffield

FRONT COVER: Sunrise over Shinjuku, Tokyo. Photo by Toyama Ken.
Design by Juan Hayward.

THE TOKUGAWA CREST: The symbol used on each chapter head and on
the cover of this book is the *mon*, or family crest, of Tokugawa Ieyasu who
established the Tokugawa Shogunate in 1603 which in turn governed Japan in
unbroken succession until the Meiji Restoration of 1868. The design for
Tokugawa's Ieyasu's *mon* is based on the hollyhock (*aoi*).

Set in Goudy Old Style 11 on 12½ point by Visual Typesetting, Harrow, and
printed in England by KSC Printers, Tunbridge Wells.

Contents

DOCUMENTS (Theme chapters):

ADDITIONAL DATA (Narrative chapters)

Japanese names: According to Japanese custom all Japanese names in this book appear with the family name printed first.
Chinese names: Pin-yin spelling of Chinese names has been used throughout with the traditional Wade-Giles system in brackets.

JAPAN TODAY

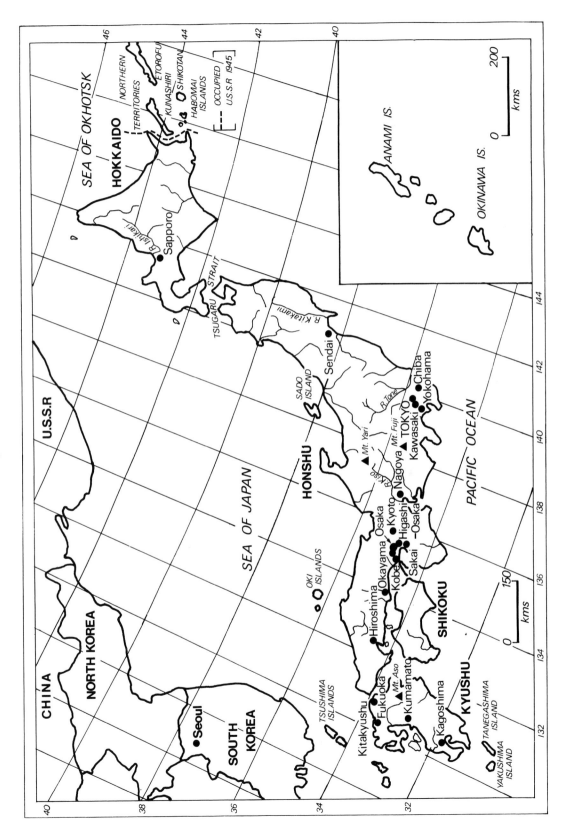

Foreword

A hundred years ago Japanese fans and ornaments were fashionable decorations in western houses. Today, Japanese cars, cameras and video-recorders are even more common features of European and American life. Both traditional and modern products show the skill of Japanese designers, but they also reflect the changes which have transformed Japan.

In the nineteenth century, Japan, like other Asian countries, was weaker and poorer than the empires of Europe. In fact, many Japanese feared that their country might fall under foreign control. However, Japan did far more than preserve her independence. She modernised so successfully that her economy is now the second largest in the free world. In many fields, Japanese products dominate international markets, while Japanese banks, shipping companies, and airlines are major influences in world trade and communication. As a result, Japan is the only Asian country to have a permanent seat at the Summits of the advanced industrial nations, and the only Asian state to give large amounts of aid to the developing world. In recent years, Japan's standard of living has surpassed that of many European countries, and today Tokyo can negotiate on equal terms with the European Community.

As rapid as Japan's industrial development, have been the social changes which have transformed Japanese life. In the 1870s and 1880s, Japan looked to Europe and the United States for teachers and advisers; and schools and colleges were built on European lines. Today, Japan herself sends advisers to many overseas countries and her educational standards are higher than those of Western Europe. In medicine, too, Japanese research and treatment have reached the highest standards, and the life of the average Japanese is longer than that of the average American or European. The Japanese may still be renowned for hard work and discipline, but many now have sufficient money to enjoy foreign travel. Until 1854, all Japanese were forbidden to go abroad, but today millions travel to America, Europe and Australasia, as well as to nearby Asian countries. In wealth, health, education and leisure, Japanese standards are often superior to those in much of the industrialised 'Western World.'

In the field of art and entertainment, Japan has experienced yet another peaceful revolution. Traditional arts, such as *kabuki* plays and the *bunraku* puppet theatre continue, but Japanese have also explored almost every art known in Europe, America and the Asian continent. Shakespeare and modern drama, rock music and the classics, experimental architecture and fashion — all are practised and admired somewhere in Japan.

The impact of these dramatic changes has not been confined to Japan and the Japanese. Many of the finest Japanese musicians are as well-known in New York as in Tokyo; and the 'Suzuki method' of teaching the violin has spread to Europe and the United States. The best Japanese films and directors have won the highest awards at European and American festivals and some American 'Westerns' have been based on stories taken from Japanese films. Japanese television programmes and cartoon films are also widely shown and admired in China, America and European countries. Japanese designers, such as Kenzo, are important in the world of Paris fashion and their products are sold in many American cities. No other non-western country has such an important impact on the world of international art, style and entertainment.

But perhaps the most impressive changes in modern Japan have been in her political system. Japan's first general election was held as early as 1890 and political parties have influenced her government throughout much of the twentieth century. Since 1945, political change has been even more remarkable and today Japan is freer than any other country in East Asia. Now Japanese can write, speak and think as freely as Americans or West Germans, and Japanese people can protest as openly as people in European countries. Most important of all, local and central governments are freely elected by all adult men and women. The creation of a free and democratic political system has been Japan's most remarkable twentieth century achievement.

Despite Japan's world-wide importance, she remains largely unknown. Few owners of Japanese cars or photocopiers know much of the people that made them. Even fewer are aware of the important influence which Japan has on the politics and trade of the entire world. This ignorance is partly due to Japan's distance from Europe and America, and the difficulties of the Japanese language. More important, it is the result of several features of today's Japan. In spite of her political and economic power, Japan lacks the strong armed forces or dramatic leaders which major states usually possess. Her self-defence forces remain relatively small and her leaders are usually members of a political team rather than powerful individuals. Furthermore, Japanese policies often reflect compromise rather than strong opinions. All these factors make Japan a difficult but not impossible country to understand. This book explores the background and historical development of this dynamic but still largely neglected country.

GORDON DANIELS *Senior Lecturer — Centre of Japanese Studies, University of Sheffield*

Introduction
Japan Under the Shogun

The Shogun with officials and advisers

Japan consists of four main islands and hundreds of smaller ones. Its area is about one-and-a-half times that of Britain, but with less useable land. Much of the country is covered by mountains and most of the population has always been crowded onto the coastal plains where the main crop, rice, is cultivated.

The exact origins of the Japanese people are unclear. They probably originated from somewhere on the mainland of Asia, which is just over a hundred miles away across the sea. Later immigrants and invaders from the mainland mixed with these earlier settlers to produce the Japanese race that we know today.

By 400 AD most of Japan was ruled by a single imperial family which, during the sixth century, became interested in copying aspects of the Chinese civilisation. From China the Japanese imported a style of government and a system of writing. At about the same time Buddhism was introduced from the mainland, and it has run alongside the native Shinto religion ever since. Art, music and literature flourished in permanent capitals, first at Nara, and then in what is now the city of Kyoto.

After several centuries that were generally peaceful the country fell slowly into disorder as private armies fought each other and defied the orders of the imperial court. War-like provincial families were employed to put down revolts, but by the end of the twelfth century they had taken over direct control of the government. From these warrior clans the *samurai* class began to develop and the position of Shogun, or military ruler, was established. The power of the Shogun, like that of the Emperor, slowly declined, and from the fifteenth to the seventeenth century Japan went through a series of civil wars as individual leaders attempted to take control of the country.

During the 1540s the first Europeans arrived in Japan. They were Portuguese, and brought guns that were quickly copied by the Japanese for use in their own wars. The Portuguese, and Spanish missionaries who arrived afterwards, also introduced the Christian religion. At first, they were successful in gaining converts but later there was open hostility towards the missionaries as fears of possible revolt, backed by Spanish troops, began to alarm the government. This led to the outlawing of Christianity and the expulsion of almost all foreigners by 1640. From then on only the Dutch and Chinese were allowed any contact with Japan, and this was strictly limited to the port of Nagasaki.

In 1600 a battle was fought at Sekigahara which decided the future of Japan. The victor was a leader named Tokugawa Ieyasu and it was his family (the Tokugawa) that controlled the country for the next 250 years. Three years after the battle of Sekigahara, Ieyasu was in a strong enough position to become Shogun. Fourteen of his descendants followed him in this post and under their rule Japan became a relatively advanced country.

In comparison with its neighbours in Asia, Japan's population had a higher level of literacy, and agricultural productivity was greater. The development of industry was quite limited but in terms of education, arts, literature and the other ideas by which the level of civilisation of a country is measured, Japan compared well with many western nations.

The Shogun's residence was his castle in Edo, the city now called Tokyo. At the same time the Emperor lived in Kyoto. He may have been treated with respect but was carefully watched by the Shogun's officials, almost totally confined to the Imperial Palace and restricted to ceremonial duties.

The Shogun directly owned about a quarter of all the land in Japan and the rest was divided into feudal domains each with its own ruler, called a *daimyo*. The *daimyo* included one group who had been vassals (*fudai*) of Ieyasu before his victory at the battle of Sekigahara in 1600, and another group who, at the time of the battle, were generally either allies or enemies (*tozama*). The country was carefully controlled and a network of officials watched constantly for any signs of rebellion against Tokugawa rule. In order to occupy their time and money the *daimyo* were compelled to spend every other year in Edo. The journey to and from their province, together with the upkeep of a residence in the Shogun's capital, and that of their own castle, was expensive and might take up half their income. There were guard posts at intervals along the main routes that checked travellers to stop arms being smuggled into the capital. They also searched for any women attempting to leave Edo, as the families of the *daimyo* were kept hostage there, though they lived in the relative luxury of their private homes.

During the civil wars there was movement between the different groups in society but after the Tokugawa took control of Japan people became strictly divided into four main classes. These were the *samurai* class, which included those from the *daimyo* down to the poorest foot soldier, the peasants, artisans and the merchants. In theory, at least, the peasants were superior to the merchants. The peasants produced rice which was the basis of the economy, while the merchants produced nothing and so were generally looked on with contempt. In practice, the merchants might well be rich, often lending money to the *daimyo*. The Shogun's government, called the *bakufu,* tried hard to keep people in their place. Lists of rules about what each class should eat, how they should dress and behave were published at intervals.

Though the system of government altered little under the Tokugawa, it was still a period of marked change. Small-scale manufacturing industries began to develop and the rigid class system was upset when some peasants managed to become comparatively rich and influential. The *bakufu* itself was forced to introduce some reforms as a result of its own economic problems and the sporadic revolts of peasants and townspeople.

Despite all attempts by the Tokugawa to control society there were those who wanted to overthrow them. By the middle of the nineteenth century the *bakufu's* hold on the country was weakened by a series of economic problems, and also because of alarm about dealing with western countries which had already humbled China. One great crisis would test the power of the Tokugawa and finally bring an end to their rule.

The village of Hakone in central Japan at the time of the Meiji Restoration

1 Shogun and Meiji (1850-1912)

Western Warships

The crisis that eventually led to the fall of the Shogun was caused by foreign pressure on Japan. In the 1850s the Tokugawa government was weaker than in earlier times, but the arrival of western ships demanding fuel, supplies and other concessions led directly to its collapse.

Foreign interest in Japan grew steadily. Russian ships began calling at Japanese fishing villages in the early eighteenth century and by 1842 the *bakufu* had withdrawn its order to kill foreign sailors who came ashore. This Law of Punishment and Warning was replaced by a policy of persuading foreigners to leave. Sometimes they were even given supplies to encourage them to go. A

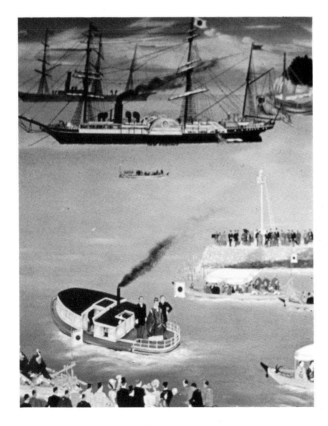

Ambassador plenipotentiary, Iwakura Tomomi, with other government leaders depart for America and Europe in 1871 to study conditions and discuss the 'unequal treaties'

2

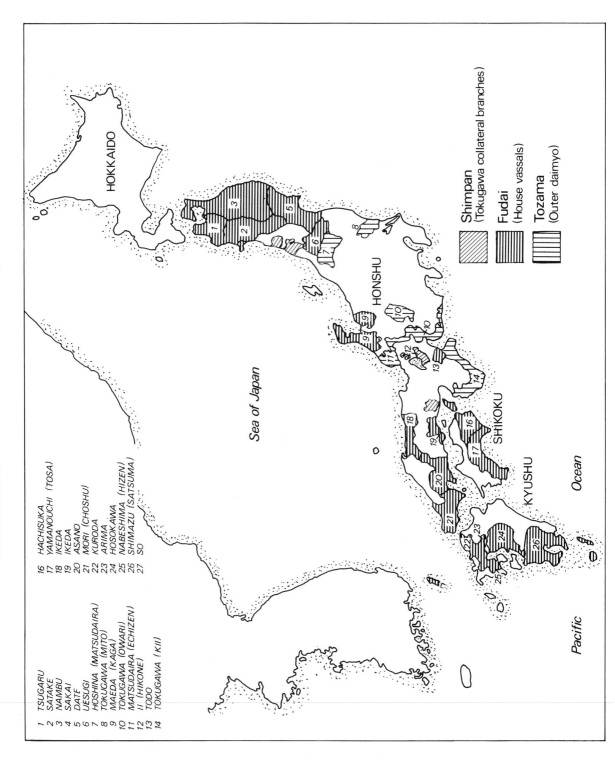

PRINCIPAL DAIMYO DOMAINS OF TOKUGAWA JAPAN

Shimpan (Tokugawa collateral branches)

Fudai (House vassals)

Tozama (Outer daimyo)

HOKKAIDO

HONSHU

Sea of Japan

SHIKOKU

KYUSHU

Pacific

Ocean

1   TSUGARU
2   SATAKE
3   NAMBU
4   SAKAI
5   DATE
6   UESUGI
7   HOSHINA (MATSUDAIRA)
8   TOKUGAWA (MITO)
9   MAEDA (KAGA)
10 TOKUGAWA (OWARI)
11 MATSUDAIRA (ECHIZEN)
12 II (HIKONE)
13 TODO
14 TOKUGAWA (KII)

16 HACHISUKA
17 YAMANOUCHI (TOSA)
18 IKEDA
19 IKEDA
20 ASANO
21 MORI (CHOSHU)
22 KURODA
23 ARIMA
24 HOSOKAWA
25 NABESHIMA (HIZEN)
26 SHIMAZU (SATSUMA)
27 SO

Japanese woodblock print showing an English couple. The Japanese artists at the time who painted European merchants in Yokohama showed little interest in distinguishing the facial characteristics of the different nationalities — hence the grotesque features

British warship visiting in 1845 was treated with great respect as it was known that Britain had recently defeated China in the Opium War.

The *bakufu* understood its weakness in the face of foreign warships. Most of Japan's cities were ports and Edo itself received a great many of its supplies by sea. Japan was very vulnerable to blockade as it had no navy and few effective coastal defences. Within Japan there were those who wanted to acquire western knowledge, and the government had some Dutch books translated to gather information. Medicine and warfare were the most important topics for study. The Dutch themselves advised the Japanese to open up the country to foreign trade. They also gave warning of British and American moves to force Japan to allow foreign trade.

American interest in Japan increased during the nineteenth century and it was the forceful approach of the American Commodore Matthew Perry, and his steam warships in 1853 that greatly alarmed the *bakufu*. Perry refused to negotiate with minor officials and insisted that the Japanese accept the letter that he had brought from the American president. This was done. Perry warned that he would return the following year for an answer, and that next time he would bring a larger fleet.

The *bakufu* asked scholars and *daimyo* for advice on how best to deal with the foreigners. This was the first time the Shogun had asked for advice on foreign policy and this showed the weakness of his position. In 1854 Perry returned and after six weeks of negotiations, the *bakufu* gave in and two ports were opened up for very limited trade with the Americans. More treaties quickly followed with Britain and Russia. Each western nation now had access to two Japanese ports. In 1856 the Dutch also signed a treaty. Nagasaki, Shimoda and Hakodate were opened to some foreign trade.

Townsend Harris, an American with the title of Diplomatic Agent and Consul-General, helped to establish further opportunities for trade. With new treaties came foreign residents, limits on import and export duties and worst of all, from the Japanese point of view, 'extra-territorial rights' for foreigners. This meant that foreigners in Japan were tried by their own officials and Japanese courts could not try foreigners for any crime. In effect, this was saying that the Japanese were not civilised enough to be trusted with judging foreigners. It was this treaty clause that the Japanese were most concerned to change as soon as possible.

Imperial Restoration

In all the early negotiations westerners had assumed that they were dealing with the ruler of Japan. They were unaware that, in theory at least, the Shogun received his power from the Emperor. In fact, Commodore Perry believed that he was negotiating with the Emperor. As foreign interest in Japan became more persistent, pressure on the *bakufu* from inside Japan became more intense. By the 1860s opposition was centred on western Japan, and particularly in the proud provinces of Satsuma and Choshu. Many young *samurai* in these two provinces agreed with the two slogans that were heard increasingly across the country, 'revere the Emperor' and 'expel the foreigners.' At this time a spirit of nationalism developed in Japan that began to replace loyalties to individual lords and provinces.

Satsuma and Choshu both tried to dominate the Emperor's court at Kyoto. In fact, Kyoto became the focus of all anti-foreign feeling. The Emperor set 25 June 1863 as the day for expelling foreigners from Japan. But the *bakufu* did nothing to enforce this and so Choshu, which had persuaded the Emperor to issue the instruction, fired on foreign ships. In another incident, in September 1862, a British citizen named Richardson was killed by *samurai* from Satsuma. In retaliation western warships attacked Choshu and Satsuma and warriors in both provinces quickly realised the importance of modern armaments and training.

The Americans arrive to sign the treaty of Kanagawa in 1854

Emperor Meiji photographed in 1872 at the age of 20

Choshu *samurai* were driven from Kyoto, and their home domain was attacked by an army sent by the *bakufu*. Included in the *bakufu* forces were men from Satsuma. They were old enemies of Choshu and on this occasion decided to support the Shogun. However, they were impressed by the way Choshu fought, and its generous treatment of prisoners. These factors later helped bring about an alliance between these two old rivals.

Choshu had modernised its army and brought foreign guns and ships. Its leaders then went on to form mixed units of riflemen. These included peasants and townsmen who volunteered to fight alongside *samurai*. This mixed force was a major break with the tradition of *samurai* armies. When Choshu was defeated by the *bakufu*, the leaders of these units refused to disband them. Later, the same units went on to seize the Choshu capital. The *bakufu* attacked again, this time without the help of Satsuma, and was defeated.

In 1866 Satsuma and Choshu formed a secret alliance. They were joined by two other important domains — Tosa and Hizen. Early the following year the Emperor Komei died. The way was now open for Satsuma and Choshu to unify the country under his young successor, usually remembered by the name Meiji (the name given in 1868 to the period of his reign).

In late 1867 the Shogun surrendered his power to the Emperor but this did not prevent some bitter fighting between his supporters and the imperial armies. In 1868 Edo surrendered but fighting went on for several months in northern Japan. Soon Edo was renamed Tokyo (Eastern Capital), and became the national capital.

The young Emperor, born in 1852, was tall, strongly built and capable. He was not, however, the driving force behind the changes which the new government brought about. It was the young *samurai* from Satsuma, Choshu, Tosa and Hizen who had helped create the new government who began many of the reforms. These leaders, Ito, Yamagata, Saigo, Okubo, and others did not immediately take high office in the government. Instead, they worked behind the scenes, as they had often done in their home provinces before the restoration of the Emperor's power. Only later did they take over important posts from princes and ex-*daimyo*.

Domestic Changes

The new government quickly dropped the slogan of expelling the foreign 'barbarians' that had helped to bring it to power. Ito and others had secretly visited the West a few years previously and were well aware of the strength of European countries such as Britain. They did not want to suffer the fate of China which had been forced to accept unwanted trade and regulations because of the weakness of its position. The new leaders realised that they would have to introduce ideas and methods from the West in order to make Japan strong enough to resist foreign pressure.

The Satsuma, Choshu, Tosa and Hizen men persuaded their *daimyo* to surrender their lands to the Emperor. Most of the other *daimyo* in the country

Members of the 1871 Iwakura Mission to America and Europe. From left to right: Kido Yoshitaka, Okubo Toshimichi, Iwakura Tomomi (with top-knot), Ito Hirobumi and Yamaguchi

followed their example. In return, they were first made governors of the provinces they had once ruled. Later, these provinces became prefectures, similar to British counties. The ex-*daimyo* were later made peers of the realm (1885) and compensated for their lost wealth with government bonds. Their *samurai* did less well from the return of the Emperor. Some, mainly men from Choshu, became officers in the army, others went into the police force or government administration. A number became successful businessmen but thousands suffered poverty. At first they were given pensions that were worth less than their original allowance from their *daimyo*. Then a small lump sum was awarded in place of the pension.

Besides being short of money *samurai* suffered other losses. Most important was the new ruling that only those in the army or police could wear swords. The two swords traditionally worn were often referred to as the soul of the *samurai*. To be without these razor-edged weapons was unthinkable. Further offence was caused by the rule abolishing the hair-style known as the top-knot. The government ruled that this should be removed in favour of a more western-style hair-cut. There was widespread opposition.

Foreign experts were brought in to advise and instruct on a variety of projects from education to railways, from banking to law. The French had begun the job of modernising the Shogun's army in the 1860s. Their advisers were replaced by German officers after France was defeated in the Franco-Prussian War (1870).

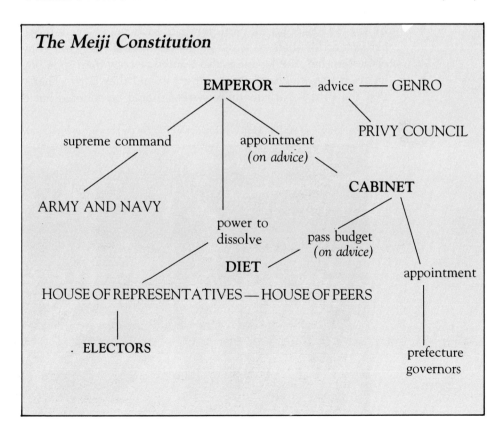

The Meiji Constitution

The British were given the job of training the Japanese navy which was largely officered by men from Satsuma. Those same men had seen the British navy at work bombarding Kagoshima in 1863 as a reprisal for the death of Richardson. The link between the Japanese and British navies was to continue until after the First World War.

Foreign experts, teachers and advisers were not employed for long. As soon as a Japanese had mastered a particular job or skill, the foreigner was quietly replaced. In 1872 a railway between Tokyo and Yokohama was completed and within a few years Japan had the beginnings of an efficient railway network. A system of compulsory education and a modern banking system were developed as well as the other facilities that were essential to a modern state. The legal system was completely changed which allowed the problem of the 'unequal treaties' to be solved. Beginning with the 1894 treaty with Britain, (which took effect in 1899) western states gave up the right of their subjects to be tried in their own courts. In effect they accepted that Japan was now a civilised nation.

All this modernisation was achieved with only two foreign loans. The Japanese did not want to depend on foreign money so they raised most of the money they needed through taxation.

Constitution and Army

Most Japanese were used to being ruled from above. Apart from the *samurai* and the aristocracy, they had little or no say in running their province or country. In the 1870s political parties began to develop even though there was no parliament for them to work in. It was natural that after copying most aspects of western life, the Japanese also wanted to copy their style of government. The question was which western country should they copy. There was a suggestion that the British parliamentary system should be adopted but this was dropped.

Promulgation of the first Meiji Constitution in 1889 in the presence of Emperor Meiji

The Anglo-Japanese Alliance

On 30 January 1902 the Anglo-Japanese Alliance was signed. The secret negotiations between the British Foreign secretary, Lord Landsdowne, and Ambassador Hayashi had lasted several months. The alliance was announced simultaneously in Tokyo and London in February 1902.

The Anglo-Japanese Alliance was the first military pact, on equal terms, between a western and non-western nation. In Japan there was a widespread feeling of friendship towards Britain as the first foreign power to fully recognise Japan's development as a modern state.

The British had been tempted to enter an alliance with Japan because she had the only strong navy in the north Pacific area that could support Britain's interests. The alliance also prevented any agreement between Japan and Russia, an arrangement that Ito had favoured.

For Japan the alliance neutralised the Franco-Russian pact. The six articles of the Anglo-Japanese Alliance stated that each country would remain neutral if the other was involved in a war over her interests in China or Korea. But if that war involved fighting two, or more enemies, then the ally would fight.

The alliance was renewed in 1905, and extended to include India among the areas it covered. It played a part in forcing the Russians to make peace after the Russo-Japanese war at the Treaty of Portsmouth. The alliance also effectively prevented a revenge attack by the Russians as its conditions were changed to make war with only one enemy necessary for an ally to intervene.

The alliance was renewed again in 1911 and continued until it was effectively ended at the Washington Conference in 1921.

Ito had visited Germany and was impressed by many aspects of its form of government. Germany's constitution aimed to weld together what had been separate states before 1871, and this seemed a good model. It was Ito who was largely responsible for the Constitution that the Emperor presented to the Prime Minister in a simple ceremony in 1889.

There were two houses in the new Diet, or parliament. These were the House of Peers and the House of Representatives. The two houses had roughly equal power. The Peers were mostly members of the new nobility, while the Representatives were elected, but only by a small percentage of the male population. The rights of ordinary people were guaranteed, but there were sections in the Constitution that limited these if they conflicted with the good order of the country.

In the late nineteenth century, many Japanese believed that one of the most important things a modern state needed was a strong army. There was a slogan at the time; 'Enrich the country, strengthen the army.' There were *samurai* in the army, but most of the soldiers were conscripts from among the peasants who were required to serve at least three years in uniform. Their effectiveness in battle was proved when one of the early leaders of the Restoration, Saigo Takamori, revolted against the government. He was concerned that government reforms seemed to be changing Japan too quickly and too drastically. Saigo was particularly angered at what he saw as a weak policy towards Japan's neighbour Korea, and he withdrew to Satsuma. In 1877 he and his followers attacked a castle which was held by government troops. After months of bitter fighting, a conscript army with modern training and weapons, defeated Saigo's traditional *samurai* force.

Further proof of the strength of Japan's new armies came in 1894 when Japan went to war with China. Both Japan and China wanted to influence the government of Korea and prevent western influence there. In the end, both China and Japan sent forces into Korea and war began. Western nations were surprised at the ease with which the Japanese defeated the Chinese forces on land and at sea. Though China was large and had a fairly modern navy its army lacked well-trained men, and all its armed forces were badly led. The Chinese were no match for the modern methods of warfare used by the Japanese, who were soon in control of the whole of Korea.

A peace treaty gave the island of Formosa (now Taiwan), the Pescadores and Port Arthur to Japan. These dramatic gains were short-lived as Russia, backed by Germany and France, forced Japan to give up her claim to Port Arthur. These three powers said that if Japan held the city this would threaten the peace of the Far East. In fact, Russia had its own plans for Port Arthur and soon took control of this important base. The Japanese were extremely angry at this 'triple-intervention,' as it was called. They had done everything possible to make their country a modern state but they were still not treated equally by the major western nations. They could not resist the pressure of three powerful western states at the same time and had no choice but to give in.

The situation changed dramatically when an alliance was signed between Britain and Japan in 1902. This meant that Japan could now fight Russia without having to worry about fighting Russia's ally, France. Once again, war was fought over who should dominate Korea. Again Japanese armies drove their enemies

Baron Hayashi and his wife photographed in London when he was Japanese Ambassador to Britain; he signed the Anglo-Japanese Alliance treaty on behalf of his government on 30 January 1902

from the Korean peninsula. Port Arthur was captured and the Japanese won the important battle of Shenyang (Mukden) which lasted three weeks and involved over half a million soldiers. At sea they defeated one Russian fleet and then completely destroyed another at the Battle of Tsushima. Now it was clear that Japan had joined the ranks of the major powers. The cost of the war was terrible. Financially, Japan was stretched to the limit and she was running short of trained troops. Thousands had been lost in battle or died from disease. Both Russia and Japan were relieved when fighting ended in 1905. Despite Japan's gains by the Treaty of Portsmouth, there were riots in Tokyo when it was learned that the Russians would not pay an indemnity to Japan to help meet the costs of the war.

Before the death of the Emperor Meiji in 1912 Japan had annexed Korea, and was admired by many nationalist groups in Asia. The Emperor's funeral was attended by officials from all the main western nations which clearly showed that Japan had become a respected modern power.

POINTS TO CONSIDER

1.   The Japanese could not resist western attempts to open the country to foreign trade. Actions by western powers in China showed that they were prepared to use force to secure trading privileges.
2.   The concessions to Perry demonstrated the weakness of the *bakufu* and provided a focal point for opposition to the Shogun.
3.   The 'extra-territorial' rights of foreigners were seen by the Japanese as a sign of their own inferior position. Throughout the period up to 1945 the Japanese were always conscious of trying to gain equality with the world powers.
4.   Western methods of warfare, government and industry were adopted with the aim of giving Japan enough strength to resist pressure from the United States and European powers.
5.   The actions of western nations in Asia, and particularly the triple-intervention, deeply influenced Japan's approach to establishing an empire in later years.
6.   The modernisation of Japan was brought about largely through the efforts of men like Ito and Yamagata who had only held junior posts within their own provinces before the restoration of the Emperor.

QUESTIONS

(a)   Describe and explain the fall of the Tokugawa and the return to Imperial rule.
(b)   Describe what you consider to be the most important aspects of Japan's attempts to become a modern state in the period after the Restoration.

2 Modernisation

Woodblock print showing station and trains of the first railway line running between Tokyo and Yokohama, opened in 1872

Introduction

In 1868 the Japanese government made clear its determination to modernise the country when it announced, in the Imperial Charter Oath, that 'Knowledge shall be sought throughout the world so as to strengthen the foundations of imperial rule.' After this the government searched for appropriate models in the advanced countries of Europe and America in industry, politics, education, law, art, literature, culture, ideas and behaviour. Some of the western fashions adopted by the Japanese in the 1870s and 1880s were temporary crazes, but the new Japan was deeply influenced by borrowings and adaptations in nearly all fields.

The great enthusiasm for western things among educated Japanese in the 1870s gave rise to the description of the period as 'civilisation and enlightenment,' and a feeling that while the developed countries of Europe and America were fully civilised, Japan was not. Eventually, this enthusiasm for western civilisation was balanced by a new interest in Japanese traditions and culture, and in the 1880s and 1890s there was a revival of Japanese values and a growth of national pride and self-confidence. By 1900 Japan was in many respects a modern state, with a constitution, parliament, political parties, growing modern industries and communications, compulsory education, a western-style legal system, and armed forces that had already defeated China and were soon to defeat Russia. However, some Japanese attitudes and ideas remained, and were mingled with ideas from the West.

DOCUMENT 1   **_The Imperial Charter Oath_**   (*April 1868*)

By this oath we set up as our aim the establishment of the national weal on a broad basis and the framing of a constitution and laws.

1. Deliberative assemblies shall be widely established and all matters decided by public discussion.

2. All classes, high and low, shall unite in vigorously carrying out the administration of affairs of state.

3. The common people, no less than the civil and military officials, shall each be allowed to pursue his own calling so that there may be no discontent.

4. Evil customs of the past shall be broken off and everything based upon the just laws of Nature.

5. Knowledge shall be sought throughout the world so as to strengthen the foundations of imperial rule.

Legal Reforms

The government considered reform of its laws essential for Japan to rid herself of the restrictions of the unequal treaties imposed by the West in the 1850s. In particular, there was a determination to abolish 'extra-territorial rights,' the system whereby westerners accused of a crime in Japan were tried by their own courts. This system had developed because westerners considered the Japanese system of justice to be uncivilised, and therefore the best way to remove this sytem was to bring Japanese law into line with western legal methods. A modern system of laws was also seen as a symbol of progress and civilisation.

In the 1870s the government set about developing a system that would win the confidence of the European powers. In Tokugawa Japan the emphasis had been on the obligations and duties of the family, and the idea of individual legal rights did not exist. However, after 1868, the principle of individual rights, and western-style court procedures were adopted. Torture which foreign observers considered barbaric was abolished in 1876. The process of creating a completely new set of civil and criminal laws proved slow and difficult, and it was only after abandoning codes which were largely based on French tradition, that a completely new legal code, based on the German model, was finally adopted and came into effect in 1907. Extra-territoriality had ended in 1899.

Transport and Communications

Japan had very few navigable rivers or good roads and so the main emphasis in transport modernisation was on railways and sea routes. Work on a line between Tokyo and the port of Yokohama began in 1870 under the supervision of a British engineer, and was opened in 1872 in the presence of the Emperor and Empress. In the early years the railways were run largely by foreign experts and workers, and trains were not operated by Japanese. The first tickets carried English, French and German translations. However, by 1880 most foreign experts had been replaced. Throughout the 1870s the system was extended, to Kobe and Osaka in 1874 and to Kyoto in 1877. By 1901 a line stretched from Aomori in northern Honshu to Nagasaki in Kyushu, and six years later sleeping and dining car services were introduced. Until 1877 the railways were under government control, but then private enterprise began to take over, so that by 1895 there were 1500 miles of private railway and only 580 miles run by the government. In 1906, the main railway network was nationalised for military and economic reasons.

Coastal shipping was one of the easiest methods of transport to develop. Furthermore, western-style shipyards had already appeared in the 1850s. Dynamic individuals, such as the former *samurai* Iwasaki Yataro, helped to expand modern shipbuilding and develop steamship services linking Japan with the Asian mainland. The government gave encouragement and in 1873 Iwasaki founded the Mitsubishi company, and established routes to Hong Kong in 1879 and Vladivostok two years later. In 1885 he joined forces with a rival company to form the Nihon Yusen Kaisha (NYK line) (Japan Shipping Company) which dominated Japanese merchant shipping until the Second World War.

One of the most interesting transport developments in Meiji Japan was the rickshaw (or jinrickshaw —literally 'man-powered vehicle') which was an ingenious Japanese invention combining strong western wheels with agile Japanese labour. Some people believe it was a modified version of the western perambulator. It first appeared in Tokyo in 1869 and within a few years there were as many as 50,000 of them operating in the capital. The rickshaw was particularly suited to the crowded narrow streets of Japanese towns and cities. The heyday of the rickshaw lasted until the early years of the twentieth century when they began to be replaced by bicycles, and later by cars. By 1923 there

Rickshaw-pullers with clients at an out-of-town location in the 1880s

DOCUMENT 2   ***Things Japanese***   *Basil Hall Chamberlain (3rd revised ed. 1898)*

Yes, we repeat it, Old Japan is dead and gone, and Young Japan reigns in its stead.... The steam whistle, the newspaper, the voting-paper, the pillar post at every street corner and even in remote villages, the clerk in shop or bank or public office hastily summoned from our side to answer the ring of the telephone bell, the railway replacing the *palanquin*, the iron-clad replacing the war junk, — these and a thousand other startling changes testify that Japan is transported ten thousand miles away from her former moorings. She is transported out of her patriarchal calm into the tumult of Western competition, — a competition active right along the line, in politics and war, in industries, in shipping, possibly even in colonisation.

1. What does the writer mean when he says that "Japan is transported ten thousand miles away from her former moorings"?
2. What aspects of "Old Japan" remained after modernisation?
3. List other aspects of modernisation not mentioned by the writer.

were less than 20,000 in Tokyo. Other forms of urban transport were adopted rapidly in Japanese cities; horse-drawn buses appeared in Yokohama in 1869, and trolley buses in Tokyo in 1883. These were replaced at the turn of the century by electric trolley buses.

The telegraph was seen by the Meiji government as a valuable tool for unifying the country and its defence, and the system remained under central government control until 1985. The first line connected Yokohama and Tokyo in 1869, and four years later an Aomori-Tokyo-Nagasaki link had been completed. Undersea cables to Shanghai and Vladivostok were laid in 1871, and by 1880 all major Japanese towns and cities were linked by telegraph. The first telephone system began in 1889 under government control, but its progress was slower than that of the telegraph, and it was not until the 1920s that its use became widespread.

The Shimbashi district of Tokyo at the end of the Meiji era. What signs of modernisation can you see?

A postal service between Tokyo and Osaka began in 1871, and by the following year most of the major cities were linked by post. The service expanded and reached most rural areas by the 1880s.

Politics

Modern politics and political parties developed in Japan as a result of two pressures. Firstly, there was a feeling that political parties, an elected government and a Constitution were symbols of a civilised nation. The most powerful countries in the world, such as Britain, France, Germany and the United States, all had representative systems and many Japanese thinkers believed that if Japan was to become strong she must also adopt these systems. Secondly, in 1874 a number of senior politicians who had resigned from the government in protest at its cautious foreign policy issued a manifesto calling for an end to the 'tyranny' of the Meiji government and the establishment of an elected national assembly. This marked the beginning of the Popular Rights Movement. Many of the movement's leaders hoped to use anti-government criticism to force the Meiji leaders to share power with them. Much of the early opposition to the government was over local, rather than national issues, and reflected hostility to a strong central government. In other words, the movement for political and constitutional reform was the result of western idealism and Japanese problems.

Hirobumi Ito — the first prime minister of Japan

The Popular Rights Movement was led by former *samurai* and its initial support was very limited. However, after about 1877 the movement began to attract supporters from a wider range of people, and soon rich peasants joined landlords and the middle class in towns in demands for national assembly elections and a modern Constitution. The government's first response to these demands was to try and suppress them, and in 1875 it introduced severe censorship of newspapers. However, the government soon set up an office to investigate the drafting of a Constitution. Like its opponents the Meiji leadership saw that the

DOCUMENT 3 *Autobiography of Fukuzawa Yukichi* (1899)

The purpose of my entire work has not only been to gather young men together, and give them the benefit of foreign books but to open this 'closed' country of ours and bring it wholly into the light of Western civilisation. For only thus may Japan become strong in the arts of both war and peace and take a place in the forefront of the progress of the world.

I was not satisfied merely to advocate it by word of mouth. I felt that I must practise it in my actual life, and that there would be no excuse if there was the least disagreement between my words and my conduct. At the same time I did not hesitate if I saw anything that was necessary in advancing the cause of civilisation whether it met with the general approval or not.

In my writing I broke with old-time scholarly style and adopted the simplest and easiest of styles.... The number of copies sold was really surprising.

I know that no scholar or writer, no matter how great he may be, could write or translate a book that would sell as mine did if he had not happened to hit the right time and occasion. After all, my success was not due to my ability, but it was by reason of the time that I came to serve.... Whatever the situation may have been, I seemed to be alone in the field of writing for popular causes, and it became the sole basis of my livelihood and later of my reputation.

1. Who was Fukuzawa Yukichi, and what contribution did he make to Japan's modernisation?
2. Why did Fukuzawa consider western civilisation so important for Japan?

adoption of a Constitution would be a further stage in Japan's progress towards western-style civilisation, and might help persuade the western nations to speed up revision of the unequal treaties. The government also saw that the ability to spread information about its policies would be strengthened by the creation of a national assembly. In 1881 it was announced that Japan would have a Constitution and national assembly by 1890.

Education and Industry

The Meiji government recognised the importance of education to create a modern state, and believed that Japan could only progress rapidly if she had an educated population. As a result primary education was made compulsory in 1872 and a start was made on developing an ambitious system of secondary, college and university education. Experiments were made with educational ideas from several foreign countries until, in the mid-1880s a centralised system, adapted from the French and German models, was adopted. This included education for all at the lower levels rising to a small number of universities for the training of Japan's future leaders. Entrance to universities was by examination not by wealth.

Foreign teachers were important in the first twenty years of education reform, but by the end of the century most of them had left and foreign ideas had been adapted to a centralised system that continued until 1945. The government did not merely learn about Europe and America from foreign experts, it also sent students abroad to study. Students had been sent to Europe and the United States in the last years of Tokugawa, and the Meiji government continued the process. Many of these students returned to Japan to play important roles in government and education.

The power of the leading western nations was based partly on the development of modern industries, such as iron and steel, coal and chemicals. The government was determined that Japan should industrialise as quickly as possible, and invested large amounts of money in the new industries. A start had been made in the last years of the Tokugawa Shogunate to develop such industries as shipbuilding, and the new government was able to build on these foundations. Despite large-scale investment in the new industries, however, Japan's first industrial revolution was built on the modernisation of traditional industries, such as cotton and silk. As in Europe and America textile factories were often manned by low-paid women workers.

Heavy industries like iron and steel were slow to develop. However, the importance of these new industries lay in the way they introduced modern methods and helped Japan to develop her military strength. In the early years great use was made of foreign experts, but as soon as possible Japanese learnt their skills and the foreigners returned home. As was common in most countries, working conditions in industry were harsh. Workers had few rights and were not allowed to organise themselves. It was not until the Taisho period that Japanese heavy industry began to expand significantly, and until the First World War silk and textiles remained the most profitable industries in the Japanese economy. By this time some Japanese cotton mills were as modern as any in the world.

DOCUMENT 4   *Social change and the city in Japan*   Yazaki Takeo (1968)

It was the bureaucrats who were most active in introducing new systems from abroad through the acquisition of new knowledge, in business, industry and society as well as in government. In their new homes the officials managed to adjust with relative ease to a semi-warrior, semi-western style of living. Applying their own ideas of what constituted 'western styles,' they set about redecorating their *daimyo* or *samurai* residences. Modes adopted from different European countries were utilised in a variety of, sometimes ingenious, combinations. A second floor was usually added, carpets put down, and standard furniture such as stuffed chairs, dining tables and chairs, and other items installed. Paper on windows was replaced by plate glass, and stoves were provided in rooms where small braziers had been standard for generations.

Money was spent lavishly in other areas to acquire western appearances. Fashionable clothes filled wardrobes, and meats were added to their diets. They took every occasion to speak English, and took carriages when leaving home. Banquets were graced by the best *saké* and had many *geisha* in attendance.

1. *Why did officials adopt western ideas and customs in the Meiji period?*
2. *In what ways did the houses of middle-class Japanese change after 1868?*
3. *Do you think that the developments described here would have been seen all over Japan?*

Social Changes

The world of the 1870s and 1880s was dominated by western countries such as Britain, France, Germany and the United States and many Japanese felt that in order to be accepted as equals it was necessary to adopt not only western science and technology but also all the other elements of western culture, from literature to ballroom dancing. The first fascination for western things lasted for about 15-20 years and during this time there was deep interest in everything from the West. Many Japanese who lived in the big cities adopted western ways, especially regarding food, etiquette and clothing.

This deep interest in the West is well represented by the Meirokusha, a society founded in 1873 and dedicated to spreading the ideas of western civilisation to Japan. The society met twice a month to discuss new ideas and published its own magazine with articles written by members which discussed politics, science, society and religion. Members of the Meirokusha expressed great enthusiasm for the West while at the same time suggesting that there was relatively little value in many Japanese traditions. One of its founders, Mori Arinori, had even suggested that the Japanese should abandon their native language and adopt a simplified form of the English language instead!

Fashion and Food

In 1872 it was decided that western dress should be worn for all court and official ceremonies, and later the morning coat became standard dress on all formal occasions. The Emperor often appeared in public wearing a military uniform in the style of European royalty. As early as 1870 western-style hair-cuts had replaced the traditional *samurai* top-knot. Japanese officials wore gold watches, carried black rolled umbrellas as they made their way to work in western-style government offices which were fitted with tables and chairs, western calendars and telegraphs.

Foreign hair-styles and clothing were no less common among fashionable and wealthy women. In the Tokugawa period it had been the fashion for women to shave their eyebrows and blacken their teeth, but these customs died out in the 1870s. There was also a reaction against traditional forms of dress, and Countess Ito, the wife of the Meiji leader, Ito Hirobumi, even proposed that the wearing of western dress should be made compulsory. In general, however, the adoption of western dress and manners was more common among men, and by the mid-1880s Japanese women were returning to traditional dress at formal ceremonies; men, however, never reverted to the old style of dress in public.

Changes in eating habits among the wealthy were also a feature of the period of 'civilisation and enlightenment.' Meat eating was condemned by Buddhism, but the Meiji period brought beef and pork into the Japanese diet, while bread, dairy products and beer also appeared. The Meiji Emperor set an example by eating meat at banquets.

Other Reforms and Innovations

In 1873 the Japanese government abandoned the old lunar calendar and adopted

DOCUMENT 5   *Address at the founding of the Kaishinto* (*Progressive Party*)   *Okuma Shigenobu 14 March, 1882*

Ever since the early days of the Meiji Era I have considered political reform to be my personal responsibility. I participated in the administration of the Restoration government and, as far as my feeble powers permitted, I worked for reform and progress. My greatest regret is that I have not been able fully to satisfy my own hopes, and that I have accordingly disappointed you gentlemen frequently in yours. Political reform and progress is the unanimous wish of our party, and has ever been my abiding purpose.

Our party is the party which stands for political progress. We wish to effect by sound and proper means political reform and progress as complete as possible. We differ categorically from those parties which fail to act when the occasion demands it, and which under the guise of working for gradual progress seek private advantage through deliberate procrastination.

1. What evidence can you find in this passage to explain Okuma's reasons for founding a political party?
2. Were there any other reasons for the development of political parties in Meiji Japan?

the western, or Gregorian, calendar. A seven-day week was instituted with Sunday as a day of rest. These changes were gradually accepted in the cities, but in the countryside the peasants continued to live according to the old calendar.

The lighting of Japanese cities was one of the most striking features of modernisation. In 1874 there were gas-lamps in the entertainment quarter of Tokyo, and four years later the first electric light bulb was seen in the capital. By 1882 an electric lighting system was successfully installed and the unlit streets of Tokyo disappeared for ever. By the end of the century electric trams, trolley buses and lifts were all in use in Japanese cities.

New Cultural Developments

Fukuzawa Yukichi

Western ideas had a major impact on Japanese thinkers, artists, writers, painters, philosophers and musicians. A key figure in spreading knowledge of the advanced western nations was Fukuzawa Yukichi, who has been described as 'the most influential man in Meiji Japan outside government service.' Fukuzawa was a *samurai* from Kyushu who had studied Dutch and English in the 1850s and had been a member of the shogun's missions to the United States and Europe in the 1860s. In 1858 he founded the college which later became Keio University. His influence was spread largely through his writings of which '*Conditions in the West*' of 1869 sold over 150,000 copies in its first edition. The book was a basic guide to the history, politics and culture of the countries of the West, and was a major source of information for many Japanese. Between 1872 and 1876 Fukuzawa published a second influential book entitled *An Encouragement of Learning* which sold almost 3/4 million copies. Fukuzawa and others like him believed Japan could only be strong if she had a revolution of values and ideas.

Literature

Natsume Soseki

One of the most important literary activities of the period was the translation of foreign works. There was great enthusiasm for the works of Samuel Smiles, whose book *Self-help* emphasised the importance of hard work and discipline, and J. S. Mill, whose *On Liberty* argued that men had rights as well as duties. By 1880 a wide range of the world's classics had been translated, including *Aesop's Fables*, *The Arabian Nights* and the novels of Jules Verne. After 1880 a start was made on the great European masters, such as Dostoevsky, Tolstoy, Dickens and Ibsen.

Japanese literature in the early Meiji period consisted mainly of realistic copies of western models. It was not until the mid-1880s that original works began to appear, from authors whose writing combined elements of Japanese tradition with western ideas. The first successful modern Japanese novel was *Ukigumo* (*Floating Clouds*) by Futabatei Shimei published in 1887-9, which was the story of an individual's search for identity in the new Japanese middle class. This novel paved the way for the works of great writers such as Natsume Soseki and Mori Ogai. These novels created the foundations of modern Japanese literature and are widely read today. The growth of newspapers and magazines provided many writers with outlets for their work and brought the new literature to a wide audience.

Art, Architecture and Music

The government encouraged western forms of painting and established the Tokyo Art School in 1876. The works produced were largely copies of western styles, but they reflected changing social life and the appearance of modern cities. The vogue for western-style painting began to fade in the late 1880s, as painters and critics rediscovered the beauty of some traditional forms of Japanese art. An American professor of art, Ernest Fenellosa, who had come to Japan to teach western art and the Japanese, Okakura Tenshin, helped to encourage the revival of traditional forms.

Western-style buildings first appeared in Japan in the 1870s and were designed initially by western architects. As the century progressed, however, western-trained Japanese architects began to take over, and were responsible for designing some of the most famous buildings of the Meiji era, such as the Bank of Japan, Tokyo Central Station and the Akasaka Palace. These buildings were all designed according to late nineteenth-century European taste, and the private homes of the rich often incorporated 'western rooms,' complete with armchairs, curtains, carpets and paintings.

An interest in western music was also a feature of the period. Students went abroad to study in European music academies, and the Tokyo School of Music was opened in 1887. Students from there were responsible for the first performance of a western opera in Japanese in 1903! Western music was introduced into the school curriculum, and many Japanese became acquainted with western musical forms and notation. An ability to play the piano became an important

A concert in the music room of the Rokumeikan in the mid 1880s

accomplishment for young ladies, but popular taste showed a broad interest in marches and sentimental ballads with western harmonies and Japanese themes.

Reaction Against the West

Criticism of excessive westernisation began in Japan in the mid-1880s. It showed itself in the reintroduction of Confucian ideas as the basis for school education. Some Japanese feared that the influence of the West would damage the Japanese character of life in Japan. Many Japanese began to question the superiority of all things western, and believed that traditional Japanese ideas remained important. In certain respects this change reflected a growing national self-confidence as well as misgivings about the future.

The history of the Rokumeikan, or 'Deer Cry Pavilion,' vividly illustrates the end of this first phase of westernisation in modern Japanese history. The Rokumeikan was a large two-storey building in the Italian style built in 1881-3 by a British architect. It was equipped with a ballroom, reading room, billiard room and music room and was opened in 1883 with a lavish reception attended by about 1000 guests. Tickets for this gala were addressed jointly to husbands and wives, something completely new at the time. The Rokumeikan was a place where Japanese and foreigners could meet for entertainment, and men and women in western dress danced to an orchestra playing European waltzes. In 1884 a bazaar was held at the Rokumeikan which lasted three days and for which 10,000 tickets were sold. The original purpose of the institution had been to show foreigners how westernised Japan was, as part of the process of gaining treaty revision. By the late 1880s the concept of the Rokumeikan was under attack from both conservatives and progressives who argued that it had not achieved its objective of ending the unequal treaties. There were also criticisms of its excessive westernisation, and in 1889 the building was sold. The 'Rokumeikan era' had come to an end.

POINTS TO CONSIDER

1.   The Meiji government was determined to modernise Japan as rapidly as possible by imitating and adapting selected features of western 'civilisation.'

2.   The government sought to obtain an early revision of the unequal treaties and this stimulated a search for a new legal system that would be acceptable to the western powers.

3.   Modernisation of education, industry and communications began in the 1870s. The education system that emerged in the 1880s combined western and Japanese elements. The most important industries until the First World War were silk and textiles.

4.   The development of political parties, an elected assembly and a constitution were seen as essential features of civilisation, and necessary to achieve international respect and treaty revision. At first the number of voters was very small.

5.   Western ideas had a deep effect on Japanese thinkers and writers and there was enthusiasm for western literature, politics and philosophy in the 1870s and 1880s.

6.   After about 1887 criticism of some of the more excessive western borrowings strengthened and in many fields a balance between western and Japanese elements began to emerge.

QUESTIONS

(a)   List some of the important ideas that Japan borrowed from the West during the Meiji period.

(b)   Why was there a reaction against the West in the late 1880s?

③ Taisho Japan (1912-1926)

Political Crisis

The period of the reign of Emperor Yoshihito, the only surviving son of the Emperor Meiji, is known as Taisho which means 'great righteousness.' The new Emperor, unlike his father, had poor health, and was unable to carry out his political duties. As a result, his son, Hirohito, ruled Japan as his regent from 1921 to 1926.

The Taisho period began with a political crisis. The Prime Ministers at that time did not have to be politicians with the greatest support in the Diet. They were usually chosen by the *genro*, a handful of elder statesmen such as Yamagata who had been responsible for creating the modern Japanese state from 1868. Prince Saionji was Prime Minister at the beginning of the Taisho period. His policy of cutting back money for the armed forces caused the Army Minister to hand his resignation directly to the Emperor. This sign of lack of confidence caused the fall of the Saionji cabinet in December 1912. Attempts to find a new Prime Minister failed at first when some leaders refused the post. Eventually, an ex-general named Katsura was appointed. He became increasingly unpopular with the people and many sections of the government. It was clear that he could not win an election so he resigned. The crisis showed the influence that the armed forces might have but Katsura's resignation showed the rising strength of anti-military opinion.

Tokyo railway station in the early Taisho period

Prime Ministers 1911-1931

Prince Saionji Kinmochi	1911-1912
Prince Katsura Taro	1912-1913
Admiral Yamamoto Gombei	1913-1914
Count Okuma Shigenobu	1914-1916
General Terauchi Masatake	1916-1918
Mr Hara Kei (Takashi)	1918-1921
Viscount Takahashi Korekiyo	1921-1922
Admiral Kato Tomosaburo	1922-1923
Count Yamamato Gombei	1923-1924
Viscount Kiyoura Keigo	1924-
Baron Kato Komei (Takaaki)	1924-1926
Baron Wakatsuki Reijiro	1926-1927
General Tanaka Giichi	1927-1929
Mr Hamaguchi Yuko (Osachi)	1929-1931

First World War

In 1914 the First World War began and by its end in 1918 Japan had established herself as a first-rate world power. The alliance that Japan had with Britain did not require her to enter the war. When Britain asked for naval assistance in the Pacific the Japanese Foreign Minister, Kato Takaaki, argued that the opportunity to gain territory at the expense of Germany was too good to miss. Despite British opposition, Japan issued an ultimatum to Germany to withdraw her ships from neighbouring waters. When Germany did not reply, Japan declared war. Within three months she had taken over all German territory in Asia including bases on the Shandong (Shantung) Peninsula of China and Pacific islands such as the Marshalls and Carolines.

The Japanese resisted all attempts by Britain and France to persuade them to send troops to the western front and to fight in Russia. Instead, they sent destroyers to act as escorts to convoys of merchant ships in the Indian Ocean and Mediterranean.

During the war Japan occupied new territory with little loss of men. As a result of the war, Japan was called upon to produce a huge range of goods for its allies. Factory production rose, foreign trade doubled, as the war helped turn Japan into a much more effective industrialised nation. Japan had to import coal, iron and steel to keep up production. Rice was imported from Korea to feed her growing population. Exports of cotton goods and raw silk, particularly to America, continued to bring large profits after the war ended.

Because Britain, France and Russia were occupied with the war in Europe, their trade with China was disrupted. As a result, Japan hoped to use this opportunity to increase its influence there. In 1911 the ruling Manchu dynasty of China had been overthrown in a revolution. The country became a republic with a president in Beijing (Peking) named Yuan Shikai. His power over the country was far from complete and Japan wanted to protect and expand her influence in China. The Japanese were particularly angered by the death of some of their citizens at the hands of Yuan's troops who were crushing a revolt in Nanjing (Nanking).

At the end of 1914 Yuan Shikai asked the Japanese to withdraw their troops from the Shandong Peninsula, as they had defeated all German forces and fighting had ceased there. This move was used as an excuse for Japan's foreign minister, Kato, to secretly present Yuan Shikai with 21 Demands concerning the relations between China and Japan. The demands were in five groups and ranged from mining and railway concessions to extending leases in Southern Manchuria — in order to strengthen Japan's position there. The fifth group of demands was the most difficult for China to accept. These suggested that China should buy half its military supplies from Japan and should accept Japanese military and financial advisers.

Yuan leaked the demands to the American ambassador. World opinion began to turn against Japan who was now seen as aggressive particularly by the United States. The demands were slightly altered and the last section was dropped. Later, Japan made further agreements with China which moderated the effects of the 21 Demands but did little to reduce the fear and dislike which many Chinese now felt towards Japan.

Siberian Expedition

In 1917 revolution in Russia brought the Bolsheviks to power. Russia made peace with Germany and this released more German troops to fight in France. There were thousands of prisoners, taken earlier in the war, living in camps in Russia who were close to starvation. There was also an army of Czech soldiers who had surrendered to the Russians in the hope of getting assistance to free their homeland from Austrian rule. They refused to be disarmed and began to fight their way towards the eastern port of Vladivostok.

The Allies hoped to use the Czechs to fight on the Western Front and an expedition was organised to help them. The Japanese sent five divisions, a far larger force than that sent by the Americans or the British. The Czechs needed no help in fighting their way to freedom. However, allied troops helped the 'white Russian' anti-Bolshevik forces for a while and then were withdrawn — sickened by the brutality used by both sides in the Russian Civil War. After 1920 only the Japanese forces remained in Siberia. Japanese troops were finally withdrawn in 1922. The intervention had never been popular in Japan and it achieved very little.

Industry and Workers

In 1918 there were riots in several major Japanese cities which were caused by the high price of rice. Prices had risen throughout the war but wages had increased less quickly. City workers were particularly affected and troops were brought in to stop the rioting. More than a hundred people were killed and many others arrested.

The Zaibatsu

The largest *zaibatsu* were Mitsui, Mitsubishi, Sumitomo, Yasuda. Their organisation varied a little, but the diagram below shows a 'typical' organisation.

A holding company controlled by the founder of the firm, or his immediate descendants.

The company bank provided finance for other company activities

The company mines produced the raw materials for manufacture

The zaibatsu manufacturing companies produced the finished goods.

The zaibatsu trading companies sold the goods abroad.

The shipping company transported the goods in their ships

Each of these sub-sections controlled several smaller affiliated companies. The whole process of production and sales was controlled by one, family-run, concern. This made the *zaibatsu* different from any other firms that existed in the world at that time.

The end of the war brought a slump in the Japanese economy as western factories reverted to peace-time production and their governments no longer required all the products that the Japanese had been able to supply during the years of fighting. The slump mainly affected the less efficient firms and many of these quickly went out of business. There was unrest among many workers, and small farmers were badly affected in 1920 when the price of rice fell by half. Trade unions became widespread but their effectiveness was limited. There were always too many workers available for unions to be very effective. Instead of large, strong unions working together, there were hundreds of small ones, usually with different ideas about how to improve wages and working conditions. Many union ideas conflicted with traditional Japanese ideas of loyalty to one's employer. The police harassed left-wing groups and so unions, as well as socialist groups, never managed to gain great influence in the country as a whole. Though left-wingers eventually won a few seats in the Diet they often argued about details of policy and their ideas appealed more to intellectuals than to ordinary people.

The war had helped develop the strength of big corporations known as *zaibatsu*. The largest of these were Mitsubishi and Mitsui. They were giant organisations with their own banks, mines, trading and shipping companies.

They were controlled by powerful families and could sell products that had been completely developed within the organisation, from raw materials to the finished article. They also had links with the Diet and even members of the imperial court. At times, the *zaibatsu* were blamed for some of Japan's social problems because of the poor working conditions in their mines and factories. They were also criticised for having too much political influence.

Alongside the *zaibatsu* there were thousands of small enterprises employing five or less workers. Many of these carried on traditional crafts and were often run as family concerns with apprentices doing much of the work. Sometimes, these small units would do sub-contracting work for the *zaibatsu*. They employed low-cost labour and were mainly involved in simple production. In contrast to the *zaibatsu* and small enterprises there were relatively few medium-sized companies producing goods in Japan at that time.

Treaty of Versailles

The victors of the First World War met in Paris in 1919. At this conference the victorious powers distributed territory taken from the defeated nations. Japan ranked alongside Britain, France and America at the negotiations and, at the Treaty of Versailles that followed, Japan was allowed to retain the territory she had gained from Germany during the war.

From the meetings in Paris developed the League of Nations, an organisation that was designed to ensure world peace. Japan had a permanent seat on the League's governing council. But the covenant of the League did not include a clause concerning racial equality which Japan had suggested. In particular, the racial attitudes of the Australian representative prevented its inclusion.

The Washington Conference

The expense of maintaining and expanding navies after the First World War caused economic difficulties for most world powers. In 1921 a conference was held in Washington to try to solve this problem. It also discussed the general situation in the Far East and the Pacific. It resulted in a number of important international agreements. In particular, there was an agreement on the relative numbers and size of battleships and other large warships. The ratio agreed for these warships meant that Japan was allowed three for every five in the British and American navies. Japan could not have afforded a long arms race with America and so the result of the treaty was not really to Japan's economic disadvantage. More important was the clause which stated that neither Britain nor America would build first-class bases closer to Japan than Hawaii and Singapore. This meant that no large fortifications were built in Hong Kong, or Manila in the Philippines. A naval treaty signed in London in 1930 extended the Washington agreement to include smaller warships.

The Washington conference brought an end to the Anglo-Japanese Alliance. After the war America's relations with Japan had been strained and Canada pressed Britain to end the alliance; she was afraid of being dragged into a war with America. The alliance officially ended in August 1923 and from then on Britain had less influence on Japanese policies.

Japan and China

The Japanese representative at the Washington conference was Baron Shidehara. His attitude at the conference was one of moderation towards China. In January 1922 Shidehara announced his China policy to the Diet. He was attempting to restore the relations that had existed before the 21 Demands had been presented in 1915. He said that Japan should respect China's territory and should not interfere in her internal affairs. He suggested that Japan should be sympathetic towards China and be patient in dealing with her. This 'soft' policy was not popular with all Japanese and helped to bring about the fall of the government in 1927. In China itself there was a growing sense of nationalism and a united Nationalist government was established in 1927. This made close cooperation with Japan increasingly difficult. In Japan many groups thought that Japanese power was the only means of ensuring that China became a modernised and useful ally.

A scene in central Tokyo after the 1923 earthquake

Earthquake

In 1923 an earthquake destroyed two-thirds of Tokyo and killed over 100,000 people. The economy of the country was badly affected and only the building industry made a quick recovery from the disaster. Recovery was helped by foreign aid particularly from America. Immediately after the quake wild rumours spread about the activities of Koreans in Tokyo. In the riots that followed many Koreans were killed and the police used this confused period as an opportunity to eliminate some famous left-wing activists.

Party Politics

Up until 1915 the Diet was dominated by the Seiyukai party. In that year a second major party was formed with Kato Takaaki as its first president. The new group was called Kenseikai. In the twenties this name was changed to Minseito and from 1924 to 1932 ruling cabinets were formed from either the Seiyukai or Minseito. In fact, governments began to appear to follow the British system of the largest party in the Diet forming the cabinet and providing the Prime Minister. The parties represented, and were largely financed by, the new middle classes which were emerging as an important section of Japanese society. In practice, the parties were weakened because they were divided into different cliques and there was strong pressure on the government from outside. The armed forces, *genro, zaibatsu* and the civil service all played a part in shaping government and party policies.

Street view of Hirokoji, Ueno, Tokyo, in the late 1920s

Besides the official groups that helped to influence the government there were several societies of patriots that were important. The most famous of these societies were the Genyosha and the Kokuryukai Amur Society. Some members of these societies were active as spies in Manchuria and China. At other times they might use violence to influence elections. Some politicians and ex-generals were also members of patriotic societies. Other societies existed whose members were made up only of junior officers, while some only consisted of civilian members. Together these societies helped encourage Japan's policy of expansion in China. Some argued for a diplomatic advance; others expected to rely on force.

Some members of these societies were influenced by writers such as Kita Ikki. His eight-volume book of 1919 suggested reconstructing Japan by suspending the constitution and limiting the wealth of individuals and companies. His ideas found particular favour among young officers from farming families who understood the poverty of the countryside during the twenties. Later, Kita Ikki was executed for his part in an attempted take-over of power in 1936.

Occasionally, extremists used assassination as a means of attempting to influence the government. Prime Minister Hara was stabbed to death in November 1921 in a Tokyo station. Though from an old *samurai* family he was not a member of the House of Peers, and so became the first 'commoner' Prime Minister in 1918. By combining compromise with good sense and toughness he skilfully kept the Seiyukai party in power. Hara's murder was approved of by some people as he was reported to be involved in a corruption scandal.

In 1924, the Minseito party took power and Kato became Prime Minister. Guided by Saionji, who was the last of the *genro* (Yamagata had died in 1922), there was some move towards a more liberal kind of government. In 1925 the vote was given to all men over the age of twenty-five. The number of voters increased from three, to twelve million. Kato also managed to reduce the army budget which resulted in the disbanding of four divisions. In practice, many of the units in these divisions were absorbed elsewhere and the army benefited from modernisation, — with new tank and mechanised forces. Some of the officers who lost their jobs were appointed as instructors in high schools. There they taught military drill and patriotic attitudes.

During this period many young Japanese men and women copied the fashions and manners of 1920s Europe and America. Jazz became popular and many older Japanese were shocked by the behaviour they saw. Beneath what seemed a very liberal period of Japanese history the police were active to control any group that appeared to be a threat to public order. Within days of extending the vote to all adult males, a Peace Preservation Law was passed that gave the police wide powers of arrest. As a result, extreme left-wing groups were openly suppressed.

A reception in the Guildhall by the City of London for Crown Prince Hirohito during his London visit in May 1921. Can you identify three members of the British royal family seated on the right?

Japan took a stronger attitude towards China. Troops were sent three times to protect Japanese nationals or strengthen defences in Manchuria. This was in response to the success of the Chinese Nationalist leader Chiang Kaishek in creating a new unified government.

During these years the Japanese army became more active in pursuing its own policies in Manchuria. In June 1928 Japanese officers conspired to blow up the Manchurian warlord in his personal train. His troops had spread into north China and the Japanese were no longer sure that they could control his activities. Instead they hoped to rule Manchuria through his son. The officers of the Kwantung army, as Japanese forces in Manchuria were called, were not severely punished for their crime.

In 1926 the Emperor Taisho died and his son, Hirohito, succeeded him. His reign was named Showa, meaning 'enlightened peace.' Some young officers and other patriots hoped that Hirohito's reign might take the form of a 'restoration' with dramatic changes to society like those that had happened when the Emperor Meiji was restored to power. They hated the *zaibatsu* and their financial and political power. The situation was made worse when the Depression hit Japan after the crash of the American stock market in 1929. Unemployment rose to about three million, there was widespread hunger and some farmers were forced to sell their daughters into prostitution to assist the family income. The inability of the government to deal with these problems led to further support for the patriotic societies and much discussion of how the prosperity and independence of Japan could be protected in the world economic crisis.

POINTS TO CONSIDER

1.   The First World War helped turn Japan into a modern industrial nation. Japan gained in terms of territory, wealth and world influence.
2.   After presenting the 21 Demands to China Japan's activities were looked on with increasing suspicion by the West. Relations with America deteriorated and the end of the Anglo-Japanese alliance brought about the gradual weakening of links with Britain.
3.   Though social conditions in Japan were suitable for the development of left-wing movements, the government remained essentially conservative. Left-wing groups were divided and under constant pressure from the police.
4.   There was an increasing pre-occupation with China in the late 1920s. Policy towards China changed and in the Depression many Japanese came to think that some kind of expansion into China and Manchuria was essential for Japan's prosperity and safety.
5.   Though two parties dominated the Diet in the twenties, they were themselves divided and the loyalties of members were often influenced by their connections with local interests and business.
6.   In the late Taisho period the services, and the army in particular, were increasingly influential. They adopted an increasingly independent line, as shown by the murder of the Manchurian warlord.

QUESTIONS:

(a)   How far was the government of Japan in the 1920s similar to that of western democracies such as Britain?
(b)   Describe Japan's foreign policy from 1914 to 1930. How far can it be described as successful?

4 Early Industry

Woodblock prints showing exterior (above) and interior (overleaf) of Japan's first spinning factory to apply mass-production techniques; it was opened in 1872

Introduction

Modern industries were first introduced into Japan in the last years of Tokugawa rule. Japanese interest in new industry stemmed from a deep fear that Japan's independence was threatened by the military and industrial power of the United States and Europe. By the 1850s both the shogunate and some *daimyo* believed that Japan would have to modernise to preserve her independence.

The US Mission of 1853, headed by Commodore Matthew Perry, further stimulated the development of modern industry. In 1853 the shogunate removed a 218-year-old restriction on the building of ocean-going ships. This decision led to the founding of several shipbuilding yards, concentrated mainly in western Japan. By the late 1850s two shipyards were operated by the shogunate and several others were established by the *daimyo* of the western provinces. In addition to shipbuilding Japanese leaders established armaments factories and iron foundries for casting cannon.

After 1868 the Meiji government was able to build on the industrial foundations created in the last twenty years of the shogunate. The progress of Japan's Industrial Revolution after 1868 was also shaped by traditional historical and cultural forces. Japan was able to use the traditional skills of its people, which had developed over several centuries, including mining, metal-working and the silk and cotton industries. Meiji leaders were able to build on their skills as well as a natural inclination for good organisation of the Japanese workforce.

Over many centuries the Japanese people had developed a tradition of loyalty and discipline which greatly helped the success of the industrial policies launched by the new government in the 1870s.

The Tokugawa reformers and modernising *daimyo* soon accepted the need for western knowledge and technology. For example, the Kagoshima cotton mill was started in the early 1860s using textile machinery imported from Lancashire. In the late 1850s and early 1860s a number of western experts arrived to give scientific and technical advice to the Japanese on modern methods of mining and manufacture.

The Meiji Reforms

The priorities of the new government were defence, national unity and prestige. A slogan of the time was *fukoku kyohei* — a rich country, and a strong military. In the first decade of the Meiji period (1868-78) there was large-scale government leadership and support for the development of basic and armament/defence industries such as shipbuilding, mining, iron foundries and communications. This imposed a severe strain on Japan's financial resources. The government took over and reorganised many industries previously operated by the shogunate and the *daimyo*. New equipment was imported from the West and the number of foreign advisers increased. By 1875 there were over 200 western technical advisers working in Japanese industry.

While the government was devoting a great deal of effort and resources to encouraging modern industries, important developments were also taking place in traditional industries. Silk and cotton goods were by far the most important of Japan's industrial products in the period before 1914. Silk accounted for 42% of Japan's total exports throughout the whole Meiji period. The most important contributions to national wealth during this period did not come from modern industries, but from relatively cheap and simple improvements in agriculture, traditional handicrafts and internal trade.

After the high-spending early years of the Meiji administration, not least in opening up and developing the northern island of Hokkaido, the government

Woodblock prints showing exterior (overleaf) and interior (below) of Japan's first spinning factory to apply mass-production techniques; it was opened in 1872

DOCUMENT 1   **_Two proposals_** by Okubo Toshimichi, Home Minister

(i) Proposal on industrial enterprises for increasing production, 1874

Generally speaking, a country's strength depends on the wealth or poverty of its citizens, and the latter is closely related with the amounts of production. The amount of production depends on whether the citizens work hard at their industries or not; however, if we go right back to the true source of that strength, we find that no industry has ever been independent of the guidance and encouragement of the government and its officials.

Let me here humbly request Your Reverence to determine a policy, study the natural blessings of our country, and carefully investigate which products are to be increased and what kind of industries are to be encouraged and concentrated on. The above policy should be to initiate industrial enterprises for increasing production, by setting a standard in accord with the people's temperament and their degree of knowledge...In this way the people would sufficiently enjoy immense prosperity. If the people enjoy such prosperity the country will naturally grow rich and powerful as a result.

(ii) Proposal on need for encouraging exports, 1875

Our plan consists in letting our merchants ship and sell our exporting goods abroad by themselves...When our merchants have obtained the right to sell directly in foreign countries by themselves, they will free themselves from the control of foreign traders staying in our country, realise the real value of fine-quality goods, and see the fact that cheap fakes do not ultimately serve for their long-term interests.

Thus the government should now take the appropriate initiative for a while, find a way to sell our goods abroad, expand it step by step so that (the government) should engage in business abroad and give example and show its profit to our merchants.

1. What part should the government play in developing Japan's industries, according to Okubo?
2. Why do you think Okubo wanted to discourage the manufacture of goods which were 'cheap fakes'?
3. What difficulties did Japan face in carrying out Okubo's proposals?

in 1881 introduced a deflationary policy and began to sell off some of its less profitable, non-military industries. These sales helped to encourage the growth of the *zaibatsu* or family business empires which became an increasingly important feature of Japanese economic life. By the middle of the 1880s the financial crisis was over.

Textile Industry

During the 1870s the textile industry expanded slowly as a result of government and private leadership. In the Tokugawa period most of the silk was produced through a simple cottage industry system. Farmers grew the mulberry trees on which the silk worms were reared then the silk was reeled on simple machinery in the homes of peasants.

After 1870 it became necessary to increase the production of silk in order to meet growing world demand. As a result a number of technical improvements were introduced. Although some important mills were built in the 1870s, most silk production continued to be carried out in the countryside as before. In the 1890s the scale of silk production and exports began to rise significantly. Technical changes allowed silk producers to introduce a summer-autumn crop in addition to the traditional spring crop. Handreeling began to decline and by 1913 72% of total silk output came from mills. Nevertheless, small hand-reeling shops did not disappear immediately. As late as 1913 there were still 184,000 in operation. Technical changes were slow in coming. Before 1914 in many of the main silk-producing areas less than half the looms were power driven.

After silk, cotton was the most important Japanese textile product. Unlike silk which was not seriously threatened by foreign imports, the cotton industry faced a serious challenge from cheap cotton goods produced in Lancashire. Imports of cotton yarn multiplied thirteen times in the years 1868-88. To meet this threat to the cotton industry businessmen and the government were forced to carry out more thorough technical changes than had been necessary in the silk industry. In the 1870s the government set up two modern spinning mills with western machinery. Then in 1882 Shibusawa Eiichi, one of Japan's most dynamic and successful businessmen, established the Osaka Spinning Mill, which was the

---

DOCUMENT 2   **_Eye-witness account of conditions in the Takashima coal mine,_** _1888_

The temperature got hotter the farther down in the mine I went. At the most extreme point it reached 120 to 130 degrees F. The miners have to labour under this heat. Their bodies are constantly covered with pouring sweat. The air is stifling and it is difficult to breathe. The smell of coal makes it almost unbearable. Despite such appalling working conditions, the company rules do not even allow one second of rest. The deputy crew boss patrols the work area, and if he sees a miner slackening his pace even for an instant he beats him with his club. These deputy crew bosses are like monsters and demons. If a miner asks permission to rest because of fatigue, or if he disobeys the crew boss, he is punished as an example to others. His hands are tied behind him and he is strung up by the beam, with his feet slightly above ground. Then he is clubbed while the other miners are forced to watch the beating. If a miner, unable to bear the harsh conditions, tries to escape and is caught and brought back he is then kicked, beaten, strung up, and generally treated in a brutal and cruel fashion by the guards. No human being could behave as atrociously (as these guards). There is no other way to identify them except to call them devils.

1. _What was the role of a 'crew boss' (oyakata)?_
2. _Why did the Meiji government develop coal production?_
3. _What were the consequences of the working conditions described here?_

largest in the country and one of the most modern in the world. Progress remained slow until the early 1890s when a rise in cotton prices, increased investment, new markets and successful leadership stimulated an expansion of the industry. In the 1890s power looms were also introduced. In 1892 there were about 900 such looms in use. By 1907 there were 9000. Although several large-scale cotton enterprises existed by 1914, in general the cotton industry like silk was largely made up of small-scale producers.

Japan's first blast furnace at the Yawata Iron Works, 1901

Heavy Industry to 1914

In purely economic terms, heavy industries played a relatively small role in Japan's industrial progress before 1914. In that year industries such as mining, shipbuilding and iron and steel employed less than 20% of the workers in all manufacturing industries. The new, large-scale industries contributed only a small amount to Japan's industrial income during the Meiji period. Heavy industry, however, had an importance to Japan which was not only financial. In 1868 one priority of the new government was defence. Heavy investment and government support were considered essential to strengthen Japan against foreign threats. In fact the strategy of the Meiji leaders created a small number of 'modern sector' industries. These industries were helped by government funds and subsidies. The capital for this heavy industrial development came from the Land Tax, agricultural surpluses and traditional industries.

The capital needed for such a programme was a heavy drain on the nation's resources. It was not easy to modify existing large-scale industrial enterprises. There was a need for elaborate and expensive equipment. The new industries required production techniques which were very different from traditional methods. Modern scientific and technical knowledge was essential. In the early years, the government used many western experts to train and educate Japanese personnel. In addition students were sent to Europe and the United States to acquired necessary knowledge and skills. In the 1870s engineering, mining and agricultural colleges were set up. In 1877 an international Industrial Exhibition was held in Tokyo. Samples of foreign machinery were imported by the government and lent to authorities throughout Japan for use as models.

To some extent it was possible to build on enterprises set up in the last years of the shogunate. All mining operations were taken over by the government and by the early 1870s it operated nine mines as model enterprises. In 1880 the Minister of Finance announced that government enterprises included three shipyards, five munition factories, 52 other factories, 10 mines and 75 miles of railways. The government also owned 51 merchant ships.

Development and progress was extremely slow in many of the new industries. In the case of iron, for example, total output in 1896 amounted to only 40% of Japan's needs. Most steel had to be imported until the government established the Yawata Iron Works in 1901. In 1913 Japan produced only a third of its steel requirements.

Mining was one of the biggest industries during these years. Coal mining in particular employed 172,000 workers by 1913. Enterprises were generally small and inefficient, however, and the cost of extracting the rather poor-grade coal from the coal fields of Kyushu and Hokkaido was very high.

The successful war against China in 1894-5 opened new markets and gave a valuable boost to Japanese industry. The war stimulated arms production and

DOCUMENT 3   *Things Japanese* Basil Hall Chamberlain (3rd revised edition, 1898)

Industrialism has leapt into existence in this land which, only thirty years ago, was divided between an exclusive aristocracy and a humble peasantry, both extremely simple in their tastes. Now almost every town has its sheaf of smoke-stacks, fifteen hundred breaking the sky-line in Osaka alone... Already the cotton-mills threaten formidable rivalry to Lancashire. Not a month passes without seeing new manufactories of cement, carpets, soap, glass, umbrellas, hats, matches, watches, bicycles, smelting works, electrical works, steel foundries, machine shops of every sort.

Formerly, the Nakasendo was an old-world trail among the mountains, the last time we travelled along the new, finely-graded carriage road, we were wakened every morning by the scream of the factory whistle...we found its silk filatures to be now its most noteworthy sight, troops of girls coming in at five every morning and working straight on till eight at night — fifteen hours at a stretch!

To walk amidst the din of sledge hammers and the smoke of factory chimneys is not to our taste, neither have we the talent to discourse of the fourteen hundred-odd Japanese banks, or of the brand-new insurance companies... which, after all, are not things Japanese, but things European transplanted.

1. What impression do you get of early Japanese industrialisation from this passage?
2. List the modern developments seen by the writer on his travels.
3. Does the writer approve of these developments? If not, why not?

the merchant navy doubled in size in two years as a result of the increased needs of the armed forces.

The world economy continued to expand in the 1890s and this benefitted Japan as well as other countries. Prices for manufactured goods rose during this period. The new technology which Japan had introduced since the 1860s had increased the efficiency and productivity of industry. In comparison with advanced industrial countries this progress was unspectacular. In fact Japan lagged behind the major industrial nations in productivity and efficiency until the First World War. However, most Japanese industries expanded continuously in the period from the mid 1890s until 1914.

Perhaps the most successful of the new industries during this period was the merchant marine. The size of Japan's merchant fleet tripled in the period 1896-1913. In 1896, the government introduced the Shipbuilding Encouragement Act to stimulate the shipbuilding industry. The act provided government subsidies for builders of iron and steel ships over 700 tons. New shipyards were opened and existing yards extended. Despite this generous encouragement Japanese shipyards achieved only limited capacity by 1914. This was partly due to Japan's dependence on imports of major raw materials. Nevertheless by 1914 half of Japan's overseas trade was being carried in Japanese ships.

Working Conditions

As in the industrial revolution in Europe working conditions were generally harsh, and wages were low. The number of workers in industry was small and the majority were peasant girls. In the early years, productivity was also low.

The majority of Japanese industrial labourers worked in textile and related industries. At least 80% of textile workers were female, often young girls under the age of 15. Women were paid about half as much as men.

At first girls from good families were attracted to the textile mills as this work was considered of national importance. But as the demand for labour increased companies began to take their workers from peasant families. The conditions in the early mills were very poor, while the factories were poorly lit with little or no heat or ventilation. Some mills worked 24 hours a day, in two 12-hour shifts. It was a seven-day week and days off were few.

In addition to wages, most factories provided board and lodging. At least 70% of female employees lived in factory-owned dormitories which were often overcrowded. Diseases were common and spread easily. The most serious disease was tuberculosis. This was responsible for at least 40% of all recorded factory deaths.

In 1893 the famous liberal reformer and supporter of industrialisation, Fukuzawa Yukichi, admitted that Japanese textiles workers received low wages. However, Fukuzawa and other influential Japanese believed that low wages were necessary if Japan was to compete with advanced western nations. A worker's wages rose with length of service and job performance. However, one of the major problems of the period was the high turnover of workers. It has been estimated that by 1900 about 40% of cotton industry workers absconded within

DOCUMENT 4 **Textile workers' song,** *early 20th century*

Harsher than prison is life in the dormitory. The factory is like hell. The foreman is the devil, and the spinning wheel is a wheel on fire. I wish I had wings to fly away to the other shore. I want to go home, over the mountain pass, to my sisters and parents.

1. *What kind of working conditions is the song protesting about?*
2. *What does the song tell you of the origins of most textile workers?*

six months.

The mining, shipyard and construction industries employed large numbers of unskilled, illiterate men in dangerous occupations. These men, usually bachelors, were organised by 'gang bosses' or *oyakata*. The *oyakata* were responsible for obtaining, housing and feeding, and organising the men in work gangs. The employers negotiated a contract with the *oyakata* who then organised his men and paid them a small wage. Most workers in the new industries were housed in barrack-like accommodation provided by the *oyakata*. These *oyakata* acted, in effect, as sub-contractors for the employers. The employers themselves often had little if anything to do directly with the work force.

The problems of poor working conditions and low productivity in early Japanese industry were closely related. Towards the end of the century some Japanese companies and managers came to believe that good working conditions have a direct influence on productivity. The years before the First World War saw the early beginnings of the present system of Japanese industrial management.

Employers began to play a more positive role in recruiting and training the workers. Some companies organised welfare schemes for their employees. In 1897 Mitsubishi established a welfare fund which provided sick pay and retirement benefits. Employers and employees shared the contribution cost. Firms began to instil a sense of belonging and loyalty in the work force. This was done by extending the idea of the Japanese family to the workplace. The firm was now portrayed as another 'family.' These moves aimed to replace fear and respect for the company with a spirit of affection and loyalty. Such firms were still in the minority but today's paternalistic attitude towards workers in Japan began to develop before 1914.

Trade Unions and Factory Legislation

Traditional attitudes of loyalty and obedience, and government intervention, made the development of Japanese trade unions slow. The first modern workers union was formed in 1897. It was the Volunteer Association of Workers. Also formed in 1897 was the Metalworkers Union. These first unions were viewed by the government with alarm. Starting with 1080 members in 1897 the Metalworkers Union had a membership of 54000 two years later. However it soon failed from a combination of government pressure and political inexperience.

After 1900 disputes continued, and reached a peak just after the Russo-

Japanese War of 1904-5. In general, however, the workers' movement had been effectively halted by 1914 and trade union organisation had made little progress.

The response of the government to the poor working conditions of the time was to announce the drafting of factory legislation to give some protection to workers. Although work began on such laws as early as 1883 it was not until 1911 that the first Factory Act passed the Diet. The Act did not come into effect until 1916 and many of its most important provisions were delayed until 1926. The Act prohibited the employment of children under 12 and a 12-hour day was laid down for women and those under 15. However, the Act did not apply to adult male workers and the inspection provisions were inadequate. Not surprisingly, the Act had little impact. It was not until after The Second World War that strong legal protection was given to all Japanese workers.

Conclusion

By 1914 Japanese industry was still largely based on traditional foundations. Industrial workers accounted for only about one-seventh of the total labour force. Most of those were employed in very small factories. Newer large-scale industries such as machinery, chemicals and metallurgy contributed only a small fraction of the country's income.

Japan's most important products were silk and cotton. They provided nearly 60% of her exports. It was the growth of Japanese agriculture and her traditional industries that carried the country through the first phase of her industrialisation.

The framework for modern industries had been laid but Japan was a minor industrial power in 1914. The First World War was to provide her with the opportunity to speed up her industrial development and become an industrial power of international importance.

POINTS TO CONSIDER

1.   Japan's Industrial Revolution was built largely on the modernisation and development of traditional industries, such as textiles and agriculture.
2.   A feature of Japanese modern industry until the early 1880s was strong government control and support.
3.   Between 1868 and 1914 Japan fought and won two major wars, against China and Russia. These victories provided an important stimulus to industrial development.
4.   Working conditions in industry were generally poor and wages low before 1914.
5.   In the years immediately prior to the First World War the treatment of industrial workers began to improve in some companies, as a search for efficiency and worker loyalty began.
6.   Trade union organisation was weak and divided throughout the period and legislation to improve working conditions developed only slowly.

QUESTIONS

(a)   Explain why the government played such an important role during this period.
(b)   Why do you think trade unionism failed to develop in Japan? Explain the slow progress of legal protection for workers.

GROWTH OF JAPAN'S EMPIRE 1875-1932

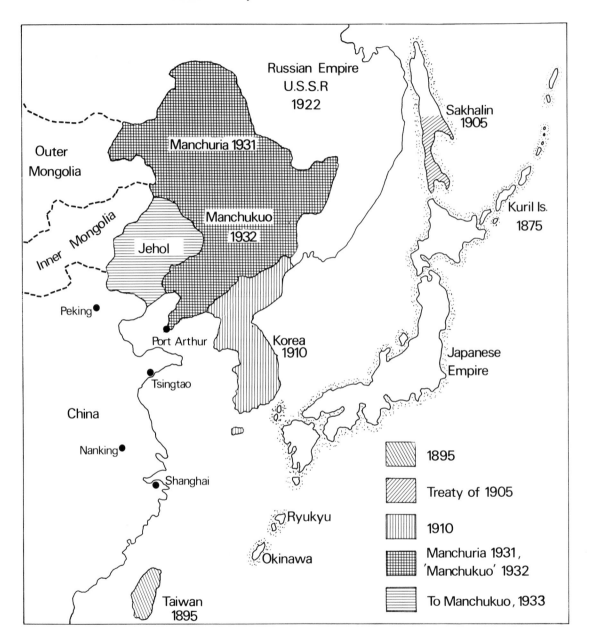

5 The Thirties

Economic Recovery

Japan was one of the first countries to recover from the world depression of the early 1930s. The government introduced measures to make Japanese goods cheaper abroad. Even in countries where the effects of the Depression were very severe the low price of Japanese exports meant that they found a market. In 1932 western nations replied by imposing tariffs on Japanese goods, or limiting imports by quotas.

The countryside particularly, was hit badly by the Depression. Taxes were high and so were the rents of tenant farmers. This led to many people moving to the towns to find work. By 1936 one third of all Japanese lived in cities with populations of at least 30,000 people. People in Japan's cities had a higher standard of living than existed anywhere else in East Asia in the 1930s, and they were much better off than the Japanese of a generation before. Between 1931 and 1936 the number of people employed in factories increased by nearly a million. A quarter of the workforce was employed in the mining, manufacturing and construction industries. By 1936 the output of mines was a third higher than in 1931. Cement, steel, electricity and coal production were also greatly increased and Japan became self-sufficient in all but the most specialised machinery. A great deal of this increased production went to make weapons and equipment for Japan's armed forces.

The Manchurian Incident, 1931. Japanese evidence of the damage done to the railway line at Mukden

Prime Ministers 1930-1945	
Baron Wakatuski Reijiro	1931-
Mr Inukai Ki (Tsuyoshi)	1931-1932
Admiral Saito Minoru (Makoto)	1932-1934
Admiral Okada Keisuke	1934-1936
Mr Hirota Koki	1936-1937
General Hayashi Senjuro	1937-
Prince Konoe Fumimaro	1937-1939
Baron Hiranuma Kiichiro	1939-
General Abe Nobuyuki	1939-1940
Admiral Yonai Mitsumasa	1940-
Prince Konoe Fumimaro	1940-1941
General Tojo Hideki	1941-1944
General Koiso Kuniaki	1944-1945
Admiral Baron Suzuki Kantaro	1945-

Manchurian Incident

Throughout the 1920s Japan steadily extended her influence in Manchuria. The area was important for its mineral resources and as a strategic barrier between Russia and Korea. Manchuria was also seen as an 'overflow' territory for Japan's huge population. Besides the 10,000 soldiers guarding the railways and Liaodung (Liaotung) Peninsula, known as the Kwantung Army, there were about a million Japanese subjects in Manchuria. Some of them were Japanese settlers but most were Koreans who were Japanese citizens. Officers in the Kwantung Army became disturbed by a series of incidents involving the killing of Japanese subjects by Chinese. Senior army men were concerned by the lack of response of the Tokyo government to a situation that seemed to threaten Japanese interests in Manchuria where 75% of all foreign investment, mainly in iron and coal, was Japanese. At the same time, the new Manchurian warlord's son was allying himself with the Chinese Nationalists of Chiang Kaishek.

Officers in the Kwantung Army decided that they had to take direct control of all Manchuria. Though the planning of their operation was carried out by relatively junior officers, there seems little doubt that members of the high command in Tokyo were aware of the plan. News that something was being planned reached the cabinet which attempted to prevent action by protesting to the Army Minister and persuading the Emperor to provide support. The Army Minister sent a letter to the commander of the Kwantung Army attempting to control him. The letter was entrusted to a major-general who was in sympathy with those planning the action. He presented it too late to stop the army proceeding with its plan. On the night of 18 September 1931 Japanese soldiers caused an explosion on the railway line just south of Shenyang (Mukden) and shots were fired at Chinese troops who were seen nearby. This incident was the excuse for the Japanese army to occupy Shenyang (Mukden), while troops from Korea were brought in to help occupy other areas.

The Council of the League of Nations voted 13-1 that Japan should withdraw its troops from Manchuria. The Tokyo government accepted this decision, but the cabinet were powerless to prevent the army from completing the occupation of the whole of Manchuria by the end of 1931.

In January 1932 fighting broke out between Chinese forces and Japanese naval units in Shanghai. This incident grew into a major battle that lasted for six weeks. In Japan a strong feeling of nationalism developed, with support for the army's actions in the face of hostile world opinion. Manchuria had a very special place in Japanese feelings as 100,000 lives had been lost there in the Russo-Japanese war. In an attempt to improve its reputation Japan created the puppet state of Manchukuo under the leadership of Pu Yi, the last of the Chinese emperors. This was supposed to make Manchuria into an independent country, but few foreign observers were convinced. The League sent the Lytton Commission to investigate, and though its report was moderate, in 1933 the Assembly of the League voted 42-1 against Japanese control of Manchuria. In response, Japan left the League of Nations and continued to follow its own independent policies.

After the Manchurian Incident, a League of Nations commission (Lytton Commission) visited Manchuria to investigate Japanese activities in the region. A report severely criticising Japanese actions was published in 1932 and as a result Japan left the League of Nations in 1933

Plots and Assassinations

During the 1930s the number of patriotic societies increased. Many young officers were influenced by the ideas of Kita Ikki and Okawa Shumei who had founded the Society for Preservation of the National Essence in 1921. Their policies were not precisely set out but their ideas were centred on a return to traditional values and the special role of the Emperor. One thing that these societies often had in common was the use of direct action and force in order to try to achieve their aims. The period from 1931 until the Second World War is often referred to as the Dark Valley. This is partly because of the assassinations and plots to overthrow the government that took place in those years.

The first plot against the government occurred in March 1931, months before the Manchurian incident. Okawa Shumei was involved in the planning of a series of bomb attacks and riots that were intended to lead to the declaration of martial law and a military government under Army Minister Ugaki. The plot failed when Ugaki made it clear he would have nothing to do with it. However, Ugaki and other senior officers were implicated and the lack of proper punishment for the plotters encouraged further action later that year.

In October 1931, the police discovered a plan to wipe out the cabinet in an air attack. Again the punishments for those involved were mild. Early in 1932, a patriotic society called the League of Blood murdered a former Finance Minister and the head of the Mitsui *zaibatsu*. In May, uniformed cadets entered the residence of Prime Minister Inukai in broad daylight and shot him in the head. At their trial they were allowed to make political speeches and they won some public sympathy because they believed they were acting for the good of the country. The most serious punishment for any of the defendants was life imprisonment.

The February 1936 Mutiny

In February 1936 young officers of the 1st Division who belonged to the Kodo faction decided to stage a revolt. They were suspicious of the circumstances behind the sudden posting of the division to Manchuria.

Copies of a manifesto explaining their motives were delivered to newspaper offices early on 26 February. The rebels surrounded the Imperial Palace and occupied a number of government buildings nearby, including the Army Ministry and the offices of the army general staff.

Groups of soldiers were sent to assassinate those who had been identified as giving bad advice to the Emperor. They wanted to create a state of emergency where the army could seize power. Two hundred rebels surrounded the house of the Lord Keeper of the Privy Seal, Viscount Saito. They broke in and found him in bed with his wife. He was shot more than thirty times and his wife was injured as she tried to protect him. One of the rebel leaders, Captain Ando, led a group that broke into the home of Admiral Suzuki. They woke him to explain why he was to be killed. He was then shot three times, but managed to survive the attack. The Finance Minister was shot dead in his home. General Watanabe was killed along with his wife and servants. Count Makino was saved by his young granddaughter after the hotel where he was staying was set on fire.

The rebels needed to kill the Prime Minister to have any chance of success with their plans. His residence was attacked and the police guards were killed. Though they had a photograph of Prime Minister Okada the soldiers killed his brother-in-law by mistake. The Prime Minister hid in a toilet until he was smuggled out of the house during preparations for his own funeral.

The Emperor was angry about the actions of soldiers of the 1st Division. He wanted the mutiny crushed quickly. Using leaflets dropped by planes, and radio messages, appeals were made to the ordinary soldiers to return to barracks. The mutiny collapsed and the rebel officers were given secret trials and then shot.

Rebel soldiers parade outside the Diet (parliament) during the February 1936 mutiny

The Army and the 1936 Mutiny

During the 1920s the success of the political parties had caused a decline in army prestige. The generally good relations that Japan had abroad meant that the careers of officers were more limited than in war-time. In addition, the lower ranks saw their families in the country areas suffering from poverty while other people in the towns seemed to be enjoying a higher standard of living. It was this situation that helped turn some officers towards the direct methods of the patriotic societies. At the same time there were groups, including many senior officers, competing for influence within the army.

One group was the Kodo, or Imperial Way, faction who wanted to stress traditional spiritual values in the army and were sure that Japan's next war would be with Russia. They saw control of Manchuria, therefore, as a step towards this conflict. Several of the most influential posts in the army were controlled by members of the Kodo faction.

The other group were the Tosei, or Control faction. This group stressed the need for a modern, well-equipped army, together with economic planning for a period of total war. They were prepared to cooperate with the *zaibatsu* provided that their policies were supported. The Tosei officers also wanted to maintain friendly relations with Russia and concentrate their efforts on expansion into China.

The most serious threat to the government occurred in February 1936 when 1,400 soldiers of the 1st Division mutinied and occupied the Nagatacho area of Tokyo that included most of the government buildings. The mutineers were led by young officers from the Kodo faction. The rebels managed to murder several important government and army officials. They only just missed killing the Prime Minister, murdering his brother-in-law instead in a case of mistaken identity.

But they did not succeed in causing a change of government. Instead, they were surrounded by naval personnel and guards units and persuaded to surrender after four days of tension. There were no public trials and thirteen of the rebels were shot. From then on the Tosei group were most important in developing army planning. Some Kodo faction officers retired and others were moved to less influential posts.

Pact with Germany

In November 1936 Japan signed the Anti-Comintern Pact with Nazi Germany. This was designed to counter the spread of communism. Italy was brought into the pact in 1937 and Spain in 1939. Japan had been politically isolated since it left the League of Nations and the pact gave her powerful friends in the West. Some Japanese, in fact, admired the way the Nazis had solved Germany's economic and military problems. More important, Japan now felt better protected against any possible attack by the Soviet Union. The Russians had already given up their interests in Manchuria by selling the Chinese Eastern Railway in 1935. There were armed clashes along the frontier with the Soviet Union, but these seemed to confirm that there was no serious threat of a Russian advance into Manchuria. The Japanese army felt that they were safe to move into China without the risk of fighting on two fronts.

Activities in China

Growing nationalism in China, which included boycotts of Japanese goods, was seen as disorder by Japan. In 1933 the army general staff decided that if China continued to act in a hostile fashion then the north of the country would have to be occupied, and a pro-Japanese administration established there. This area was to be particularly useful to Japan as it had important natural resources, including large deposits of iron-ore. In 1933 Jehol province was taken and incorporated into Manchukuo. Hebei (Hopei) province was also attacked and Japan soon dominated the whole of North China with a demilitarised zone that stretched from the borders of Manchukuo to Beijing (Peking).

The Government

The army had an increasing influence within the government in the 1930s. But it never directly controlled the country in the way that the Nazis controlled life in Germany. Even so, there was a shift away from the party-dominated government of the 1920s to one where the army could cause the resignation of any cabinet and also help choose its members. Plots and assassinations meant that party members might risk their lives if they opposed army actions openly.

In the 1930s there was no real change in the structure of the political institutions that had been developed under the Meiji Constitution, and there was no change to the Constitution itself. There was only a change in the influence of the groups within the government. The liberal trends of the 1920s were largely reversed. Many people had begun to reject the party system which seemed to be foreign and was no longer able to deal effectively with Japan's problems.

Within the existing system of government the cabinet had wide-ranging powers. For example, it could dissolve the Diet, interfere in elections, limit freedom of speech and control the information that reached the people. However, the army vetoed cabinet appointments that they did not approve of, and later nominated men of their own choice for cabinet posts. The influence of the two main parties dwindled, and though there were members of both Minseito and Seiyukai in the cabinet formed in May 1932, they were expected to put aside their party loyalties when they entered the government.

Though the parties could no longer form a cabinet, or even have great influence within one, their support was still important as they controlled the Lower House of the Diet to which elections still took place. In April 1937 the Minseito and Seiyukai parties joined forces and won an overwhelming victory. The result was that Prime Minister, ex-general Hayashi, was forced to resign. The people had shown by their votes that they rejected the idea of a one-party state. To resolve a difficult situation and unite the country, Prince Konoe became Prime Minister. He was a popular choice for some groups but within a month Japan was engaged in a full-scale war with China.

POINTS TO CONSIDER

1.   In the 1930s there was little, or no, change to the political institutions that had been set up by the Meiji constitution. There was only a shift in the balance of influence between groups involved in the government.
2.   Japan was not ruled by the military in the 1930s, but they did have great influence in deciding policy and choosing members of the cabinet.
3.   The army was split into two main factions with different ideas on the foreign policy Japan should follow. After the mutiny in 1936 major planning was concerned with expanding into China, rather than war with Russia.
4.   The political parties in the Lower House had less influence in the 1930s than in the previous decade, but they were never suppressed in the way that parties were in Nazi Germany at that time.
5.   The expanding industries of the 1930s needed the raw materials that were available in Manchuria and North China.
6.   The mild punishments of many of those who plotted against the government, or carried out assassinations, helped encourage others to follow their example.

QUESTIONS:

(a)   Why was the army allowed so much freedom of action in the 1930s?
(b)   Describe the plots and assassinations that took place in the 1930s, and explain their importance in the history of the period.

⑥ Education

Introduction

Japan has a long history of study and education. This is largely because Confucian thinkers believed that study improved people's minds and behaviour. In the Tokugawa period people slowly became richer, and more and more Japanese sought to obtain education. The shogunate and local lords established schools for *samurai* and by the middle of the nineteenth century there was at least one official school in each of the domains (*han*).

There were three types of education in Tokugawa Japan. Firstly, there were the official schools which were run for the sons of *samurai*. These emphasised the Chinese classics, elegant writing, ethics and martial arts. They also stressed physical training and fitness and aimed to train young members of the *samurai* class as warriors and administrators. Secondly, there were private academies many of which encouraged new ideas. In the early eighteenth century 'Dutch' or 'Western' learning began in some of these private schools. Finally, there were 'temple schools' for common people. These taught reading, writing and simple mathematics, as well as the rules of good behaviour.

The Tokugawa government encouraged education for several reasons. Firstly, the idea of learning was an important part of the Confucian tradition. Secondly,

A 'terakoya' or village school in the Tokugawa period

education, and especially moral education, was thought important to preserve the peace of the country. Finally, education was a useful means of training able officials.

By the 1860s, about 40% of boys and about 10% of girls were receiving some education outside the home. Many others received basic education within the home. As a result, Japan's literacy rate was the highest in Asia and higher than in many European countries.

Tokugawa education contributed two important traditions to Japan. On the one hand, many people recognised the importance of study for the welfare of the country; and education helped people to accept new ideas. As in Europe advanced education was provided for political and military leaders. However, many Japanese merchants and peasants were eager for a simple education which would help them in everyday life.

Meiji Education

From the beginning, the Meiji leaders recognised the importance of education in developing a modern nation. They believed that everyone should be educated and that the government should provide every Japanese with basic education.

In the first twenty years of the Meiji period the Japanese government looked abroad for educational methods which would be suitable for Japan. For a time in the 1870s, American, French and German ideas attracted a lot of interest. During these years a considerable number of foreign teachers and advisers were employed; and most official textbooks and school subjects were copied from western models.

In 1871 a Ministry of Education was established to supervise the development of a modern education system. The next year the Fundamental Code of Education sought to make primary education compulsory for all Japanese between the ages

CHANGES IN THE ENROLMENT RATE IN COMPULSORY EDUCATION

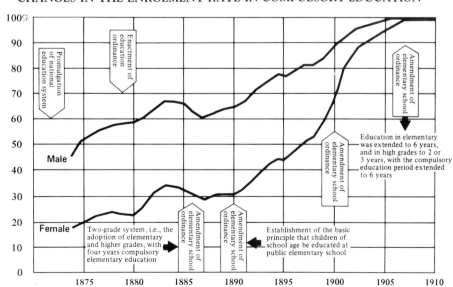

DOCUMENT 1   *Letter from Mori Arinori,* then Japanese minister in the United States, to Theodore Woolsey, ex-president of Yale College, 3 February 1872

Dear Sir,

Having been especially commissioned, as part of my duty in this country, to look after the educational affairs of Japan... I desire to obtain from you a letter of advice and information upon this subject, to assist my countrymen in their efforts to become instrumental in advancing civilisation in the East. In a general way I wish to have your views in reference to the elevation of the condition of Japan, intellectually, morally, and physically, but the particular points in which I invite your attention are as follows:

The effects of education –

1. upon the material prosperity of the country;
2. upon its commerce;
3. upon its agricultural and industrial interests;
4. upon the social, moral, and physical condition of the people, and –
5. its influences upon the laws and government.

Information on any one, if not all, of these points, will be gratefully received and appreciated by me, and the same will soon be published, both in the English and Japanese languages, for the information of the Japanese Government and people.

Yours respectfully,

Your obedient servant,

Mori Arinori

1. Who was Mori Arinori? What position did he hold (a) at the time this letter was written, and (b) in later years?

2. What evidence is there in this passage that Mori thought a modern education system was important for Japan? Find details in the chapter on 'Education' that support this view.

of 6 and 14. This was to be done by establishing over 50,000 primary schools throughout the country. There was a plan to set up 256 secondary or middle schools and eight universities. This vast scheme faced many practical difficulties, and by 1902 there were still only two government universities, 222 middle schools and just over 27,000 primary schools.

The government lacked money, suitable buildings and teachers, and there was a shortage of funds for the new education system. At this time large amounts of government money were used for industry and the army and navy. For many years truancy was high; in fact, in 1878 school attendance was only about 40%. By 1900, however, attendance had risen to over 90%. In rural areas, in particular, there was often opposition to the new schools. This was understandable, because although primary education was made compulsory under the new law, it was not free. Furthermore, some peasants thought education lacked practical value. Protests against schools and school officials were common in country areas well into the 1880s.

The 1872 Code required four years of compulsory education. In 1879 this was reduced to sixteen months between the ages of six and 14, with at least sixteen weeks of school attendance each year. In 1886 the requirement was raised to four years and finally in 1907 to six years. In the 1880s some Meiji leaders began to criticise ideas and attitudes introduced from the West. The content of education became more patriotic and the importance of moral education was emphasised.

One of the most important figures in Meiji education was Mori Arinori who had lived and travelled in Europe and America. In 1885 Mori was appointed Minister of Education, and introduced a number of reforms which established the basic educational structure of Japan for the next 70 years. Mori's most important idea was that education should serve the interests of the state. He achieved this by following French and German patterns, organising a centralised system with government control over school subjects, teacher training, and textbooks.

The process of creating a 'Japanese' education system was largely completed by the time of Mori's murder in 1889. The following year saw the publication of the Imperial Rescript on Education. This was an important statement which emphasised the value of Confucian ideas of obedience and cooperation and stressed the idea of loyalty to the Emperor. It ended twenty years of change and experiment in education. Until 1945, the reading of the Imperial Rescript, like bowing to the portrait of the Emperor, was a central feature of many ceremonies in schools.

Mori Arinori

The system established by Mori combined elements from different western systems with Japanese and Confucian elements. From France and Germany came the idea of a centralised state system; from Germany the system of higher education built around a small number of high quality universities; and from the United States many teaching ideas and an interest in vocational education. These ideas

DOCUMENT 2   **_Unbeaten Tracks in Japan_**   _Isabella Bird (1878)_

The village of Irimithi, which epitomises for me at present the village life of Japan, consists of about three hundred houses built along three roads. Down the middle of each a rapid stream runs in a stone channel, and this gives endless amusement to the children...But at 7a.m. a drum beats to summon the children to a school whose buildings would not discredit any school-board at home. Too much Europeanised I thought it, and the children looked very uncomfortable sitting on high benches in front of desks, instead of squatting, native fashion. The school apparatus is very good, and there are fine maps on the walls. The teacher, a man about twenty-five, made very free use of the blackboard, and questioned his pupils with much rapidity. Obedience is the foundation of the Japanese social order, and with children accustomed to unquestioning obedience at home the teacher has no difficulty in securing quietness, attention, and docility....The younger pupils were taught chiefly by object lessons, and the older were exercised in reading geographical and historical books aloud....Arithmetic and the elements of some of the branches of natural philosophy are also taught.

...I understood the teacher to say that detention in the school house is the only punishment now resorted to....When twelve o'clock came the children marched in orderly fashion out of the school grounds, the boys in one division and the girls in another, after which they quietly dispersed.

1. What European features did the writer find in the school she visited?

2. In what ways did Japanese culture help to ensure discipline in the school?

3. From what you know of early modern education in Japan, do you think this was a typical village school?

were developed within a blend of Confucian and Japanese values, such as loyalty and the uniqueness of the Japanese state.

In 1886 the first imperial university, Tokyo, was established. This became the most important educational institution in the country. Between 1886 and 1918 four more imperial universities were established, with Kyoto ranking second in prestige. A considerable degree of academic freedom was allowed in universities.

The imperial universities pursued higher learning and research, and were institutions for Japan's élites. This group was created by means of fierce competition in examinations. The small number of imperial universities produced a struggle for places that was highly competitive. Entrance examinations rather than money played a central role in the system. To win a place at the best middle school or university required great determination and hard study. In addition to the imperial universities run by the government, there were private universities. The most important and influential of these were Keio and Waseda. Until 1918, however, only the imperial universities had full university status.

In the 1880s it was decided that each prefecture would have an 'ordinary' middle school and that the country should have five 'higher' middle schools. It was well known that the way to Tokyo Imperial University was through the Tokyo First Middle School and the First Higher School. The middle schools were for boys only. Only about 20% of students from the ordinary middle schools were able to advance to the 'higher' middle schools. There were about 40,000 students in public secondary education at the end of the century and between 1900 and 1935 enrolment in secondary schools increased significantly.

In the late Meiji period there was a significant development in practical education for work partly influenced by American ideas and the new needs of the Japanese economy. A Vocational Education Law was passed in 1894, and soon fishery, forestry, agriculture and other vocational schools were established at the lower secondary level. For girls, there were special schools of sewing, midwifery and nursing. The early years of the twentieth century saw the emergence of special schools (*semmongakko*) and higher technical schools in commerce, engineering and other subjects. These schools trained many doctors, dentists, accountants and engineers. Practical education of this sort was generally considered inferior to the education available at imperial universities. However, the engineering department of Tokyo Imperial University was very highly regarded.

Yasuda Auditorium, Tokyo University today

Imperial College of Engineering, Tokyo, in the late 1870s

Women's Education

At the elementary school level boys and girls were educated together. However, education for boys and girls followed different paths at the secondary level. While boys went on to middle schools, girls were educated in 'girls' high schools' which emphasised manners, ethics for women, home economics, child care, and sewing. In 1894 there were 13 such schools with only 2000 pupils, and most secondary education for girls was provided in private schools, many run by missionaries. Towards the end of the century, however, the expansion of the economy forced the government into taking a greater interest in secondary education for girls, and the number of 'girls' high schools' started to increase. In 1900 a medical school for girls was opened. The following year the Japan Women's University began and soon afterwards a small number of women students were admitted to the Tohoku Imperial University in Sendai. Despite these changes, most university students were men.

*A pre-Meiji text book
(mathematics)*

Ideology

From 1890 to 1945 government ideas of loyalty were central to much of the school system. The government projected Japan as a unique family state, and the father of this 'family' was the Emperor who was the symbol of the nation and its unity. Ideas of loyalty, respect and obedience to teachers and leaders were strongly stressed in most school subjects, especially in geography, history and ethics. Ceremonies connected with the portrait of the Emperor and the Imperial Rescript, and stories of the lives of Japanese heroes served to reinforce the official ideology. The nationalism and militarism of the 1930s saw more extreme examples of official propaganda. Military training became common in many schools.

The imposition of such doctrines was much more difficult at university level. Radical ideas and attitudes were a feature of many of the private universities before the First World War. After 1918 the imperial universities were often centres of new, experimental ideas.

From Taisho to 1945

Educational opportunities increased rapidly after 1918. The number of universities increased from 5 to 46 between 1918 and 1930. The number of students in colleges and universities multiplied two-and-a-half times in the period 1915 to 1925, and liberal and even Marxist ideas flourished in the universities. These changes had little effect on the lower levels of education. However, the 1918 edition of the ethics textbook reflected some liberal ideas.

In the 1930s as Japan became involved in war with China, even the academic freedom of the universities came under attack and some professors holding views opposed to official ideas were removed from their posts. After 1937 Japanese universities increasingly fell under the influence of government thinking. The idea of loyalty to the Emperor was emphasised more strongly at virtually all levels of education.

Between 1938 and 1941 a number of reform proposals were made. These included the extension of compulsory elementary education to eight years, and five years of compulsory part-time education for those who only completed their elementary education. There was to be a common system for secondary schools and the establishment of high schools and universities for women.

The Second World War expanded scientific and technical education. In this sense the war period laid some of the foundations of the post-war education system.

Few of the planned reforms were put into practice during the war. In 1938 many students were mobilised into the armed forces and in 1944 into factories and agriculture. Air raids destroyed schools and interrupted classes. By the end of the war virtually all education was at a standstill.

Post-war Education

The American authorities and many Japanese liberals believed that the pre-war system of education was undemocratic and had contributed to the rise of aggressive patriotic policies in Japan. They aimed to make the system more democratic and to free it from tight central control. The 1947 Fundamental Law of Education emphasised democracy, individuality, peace and truth.

DOCUMENT 3   ***Traveller from Tokyo***   John Morris (1943)

Nothing could be more different from Oxford and Cambridge than a Japanese university....The building was suggestive of a prison rather than a university, and seemed not to have been cleaned since the day it was built. The windows were thick with grime and difficult to open....There was an iron stove in one corner of the room and a pile of firewood, but never anyone to light it. The feeling that one had entered a prison was further enhanced by the sight of the students, with their closely-shaven heads and their dingy black uniforms.

The oustanding merits of the Japanese educational system are that it is both cheap and democratic. There is none of the snobbery that is such a marked feature of our English educational system, the schools and universities being open to all without regard to wealth or class.

Military training is now compulsory in all Japanese schools and universities, including even the Academies of Art and Music. Every educational institution in the country has a number of army officers attached to it....They are in theory subordinate to the principal of the school, but in actual practice they have a great deal of power.... The military instruction includes lectures on discipline and the merit in dying for one's country. I have no hesitation in saying that military training is the most unpopular feature of Japanese school life. Every student I knew loathed it and would seize eagerly upon the slightest opportunity to avoid attendance.

1. In what ways does the writer consider the Japanese education system superior to the British?
2. What evidence is there to suggest that this is a description of education in the late 1930s?
3. What features of the situation described here would you find in Japan today?

The American educational mission of 1946 proposed reorganisation along largely American lines. But Japanese liberals also exerted an important influence. Compulsory education was to be extended to nine years, and a uniform 6-3-3-4 system would be introduced; that is, 6 years of elementary education, 3 years of lower secondary school, 3 years of upper secondary school and 4 years of university. There was to be coeducation at all levels, an expansion of college and university education and local control over schools. To carry out these reforms an American official was sent to each prefecture to supervise progress. Nevertheless, Japanese officials played an important role in shaping the details of reform.

The new programme faced many problems. The war had destroyed about one third of Japanese schools, and there was a shortage of funds and teachers. The Occupation authorities had demanded the removal of extremist patriotic teachers. Finally, all pre-war textbooks were withdrawn and the teaching of history and geography was stopped until new textbooks were prepared. The ethics course was abandoned.

Higher education mushroomed again. The number of universities rose from 49 in 1942 to 245 in 1955. The number of university students increased by 450% in the years 1950 to 1970. Although educational opportunities increased rapidly after the war, many problems remained. In some new universities the quality of education was relatively low. Tokyo University, formerly Tokyo Imperial

---

DOCUMENT 4   ***Fundamental Law of Education 1947 EXCERPTS***

Having established the Constitution of Japan, we have shown our resolution to contribute to the peace of the world and welfare of humanity by building a democratic and cultural state. The realisation of this ideal shall depend fundamentally on the power of education. We shall esteem individual dignity and endeavour to bring up people who love truth and peace, while education which aims at the creation of culture, general and rich in individuality, shall be spread far and wide....

ARTICLE 1 *Aim of education.* Education shall aim at the full development of personality, striving for the rearing of the people, sound in mind and body, who shall love truth and justice, esteem individual value, respect labour and have a deep sense of responsibility, and he imbued with the independent spirit, as builders of a peaceful state and society.

ARTICLE 2 *Educational principles.* The aim of education shall be realised on all occasions and in all places. In order to achieve the aim, we shall endeavour to contribute to the creation and development of culture by mutual esteem and cooperation, respecting academic freedom, having a regard to actual life and cultivating a spontaneous spirit.

1. *What democratic features can you see in the new education system?*
2. *How do the aims and principles of the new education system differ from the pre-war system?*
3. *Read Document 1 again and explain the differences between the role of education in 1872 and 1947.*

University, retained its status and position as the country's leading institution. All the national universities and most private universities were opened to women.

The control of education by the Ministry of Education was blamed for encouraging pre-war aggressive nationalism. The Occupation authorities tried to give more power to local areas through elected committees. Since 1952, however, the Ministry of Education has reestablished much central control over the education system.

In June 1947, the Japan Teachers' Union was created. For the first time teachers in Japan had a nationwide organisation to protect their interests. Since 1952 the left-wing union has been in almost continuous conflict with the Ministry of Education over the content and control of public education.

JAPAN'S POST-1945 SCHOOL SYSTEM

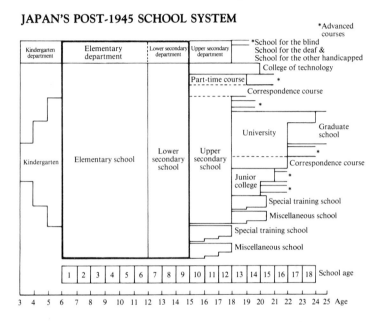

Japanese Education Today

Today the Japanese are probably the most education-conscious people in the world. In 1983 nearly 30 million out of the population of 120 million were involved in some type of formal education. In addition, there is an enormous variety of part-time education.

All children between the ages of 6 and 15 attend 6-year elementary schools and 3-year lower secondary schools. Students can then choose to leave school or go on to upper secondary education. In 1986 over 94% of lower secondary school graduates entered upper secondary schools or technical colleges. Almost 40% of upper school graduates continued into higher education. In 1987 Japan had 460 universities (plus a University of the Air), of which 329 were private colleges and universities. Many private universities receive financial help from the government. The number of university students reached almost 1.9 million.

Education is recognised as vitally important to Japanese economic success and the remarkable stability of Japanese society. To ensure a successful career in

Junior co-educational high school class

government or business it is considered essential to go to one of the best universities. This has been the case since the beginning of the modern education system. If anything, competition has become more severe since the war and there is a generally-accepted ranking of universities with Tokyo at the top. Former imperial universities such as Kyoto and Kyushu are next, along with the leading private universities such as Keio, Waseda, Doshisha and Sophia. The other national and public universities follow. National universities like state universities in America have relatively low fees. The best jobs are generally only available to graduates from the top universities. For example in 1978 nearly 89% of senior officials in the Ministry of Finance and 76% in the Ministry of Foreign Affairs were graduates of Tokyo University. To enter university a student has to pass

Learning with computers at an elementary school

the entrance exam of the university of his choice. These examinations take place in February and March each year and have given rise to the phenomenon known as 'examination hell.' Students who fail the entrance exam often enrol in special cramming schools to prepare themselves to re-sit the entrance exam. The physical and emotional pressures of this system can be very severe indeed.

In April 1986 the Japanese government published the first of several reports on educational reform. The report spoke of 'schools in crisis' and suggested that the education system had become an 'educational wasteland.' However, in comparison with the problems of education in many western countries, most of Japan's educational problems seem small. Some of the problems highlighted by the report included bullying in schools and the entrance examination system. But these problems can also be found in other advanced countries. As in many countries, education is an important political issue, and arguments about the educational system are likely to continue.

Education has made an important contribution to the development of modern Japan. The Meiji leaders recognised the importance of an educated society in the modernisation of the country and developed a centralised system built around a number of high-quality universities. Post-war Japanese governments have created a much more open and democratic system, but the pre-war features of considerable central control and the ranking of universities remain.

DOCUMENT 5 **National Council on Educational Reform** *Second report on educational reform (April 1986) EXCERPTS*

In 1973, as the post-war push for rapid rebuilding and growth slowed and the nation entered a period of transition, the Central Council for Education made several ambitious recommendations. In the decade or so since, however, these have not been implemented, due to the resistance of educators and administrators who wished to maintain the status quo.

We must face the harsh reality of the problem in our schools and the serious state of dilapidation or 'desolation' of our educational system which they signal.

The state of desolation in education implies desolation in children's minds. The whole of adult society is responsible for the deep-rooted causes which have brought this about. The diseases of adult society which have made wastelands of children's minds are closely related to our delay in recognising and dealing with the negative side-effects of modern industrial civilisation, our drive to 'catch up' in modernisation, and the high level economic growth of Japan, in particular the adverse effects of these social changes on our mental and physical health, as well as their cultural and educational ramifications.

1. Why were the 1973 reform recommendations not carried out? Are there other reasons in addition to those given in the document?
2. What are some of the negative aspects of the modern education system?
3. The present education system has been very successful in creating a highly educated population who have contributed to the post-war economic miracle. Why, therefore, does the report think changes are so important?

POINTS TO CONSIDER

1.   Japan has a strong tradition of education and important changes in the Tokugawa period laid the framework for the development of a modern education system by the Meiji government.

2.   The Meiji government saw the importance of compulsory mass education in building a modern country. The search for an appropriate model lasted 20 years, and produced a centralised system combining foreign and Japanese elements.

3.   A system of elite universities was developed to serve the interests of the country and to train Japan's future leaders. As in most countries, the rigid discipline of the lower levels of education was not exercised in higher education.

4.   The quantity of educational opportunities expanded after the First World War. In the 1930s patriotic and military ideas became influential in all levels of education, and after 1937 even the universities were influenced by government policy.

5.   The Occupation authorities considered that pre-war education had been partly responsible for the growth of militarist ideas. They tried to make the new system more democratic, and transfer the responsibility for education to local education boards. After 1952, however, central control of education was partly revived.

6.   Japan is a very education-conscious country. A vast range of educational opportunities are available and at least a quarter of the population is involved in education at some level. In the 1980s an education debate is underway discussing how the system should be adapted to meet changing needs and circumstances.

QUESTIONS

(a)   What was the role of education in the modernisation of Japan?
(b)   How different is education now from pre-war patterns?

7 Japan at War (1937-1945)

War in China

On the night of 7 July 1937 fighting broke out between Japanese and Chinese troops at the Marco Polo Bridge near Beijing (Peking). The incident was unplanned but the fighting soon spread. Both sides seem to have expected a negotiated settlement but both reinforced their troops to strengthen their positions. A growing sense of nationalism made Chinese resistance more stubborn than before and Japanese were exasperated by anti-Japanese movements in China.

The Japanese cabinet wanted a settlement of the conflict in China but some army officers argued that Chiang Kaishek's government should be crushed before it could fully unite China, or perhaps make an alliance with the Soviet Union. Closer links between China and Russia seemed possible as Chiang had reached an agreement with the Chinese communists a few months before. This agreement was designed to end internal conflict and lead to united Chinese opposition to Japan.

Japanese pre-radar sound detectors for locating enemy aircraft

The Japanese army had no detailed plans for a general war in China, against its 400 million people. Their preparations had mainly been concerned with the possibility of fighting Russia. Russia had more troops in the Far East in 1937 than Japan had in Manchuria. The strategic planning of Japan's army sought to create a buffer-zone in North China that would protect Manchuria from any surprise attack from the south during a war with Russia.

In the summer of 1937 few Japanese officers were worried about any immediate invasion of Manchuria from the north. This meant that involvement in a full-scale war in China seemed to be a safe option. In August fighting between Japanese and Chinese forces broke out in Shanghai. This developed into a bitter struggle that lasted three months. The Chinese appealed to the League of Nations and Japan refused to attend an international conference in Brussels which aimed to bring about a settlement. Japanese aggression was condemned by the League of Nations and by much of world opinion. Japanese advances continued. Beijing (Peking) and Tianjin (Tientsin) were soon under Japanese control, and in December Chiang's capital, Nanjing (Nanking), was taken. The capture of the city was followed by the killing of a great many Chinese civilians. News of these events was not allowed to appear in newspapers in Japan but was widely reported in other countries. The behaviour of the Japanese army in China, together with the sinking of the US warship, *Panay*, did considerable damage to Japan's relations with America.

Women sewing 'senninbari' (soldiers amulets)

The Japanese expected Chiang to make peace once he had lost his capital, but instead he fought on. The coast of China was blockaded to prevent war supplies from reaching the Chinese and a further offensive was launched to force them to give in. By October 1938, Hankou (Hankow) and Guangzhou (Canton) were captured but Chiang rejected all offers to make peace. The Japanese army controlled many Chinese cities while communist guerilla units were able to operate freely in many country areas. The war was becoming increasingly costly to Japan but there was no question of withdrawing troops without first reaching a settlement that was to Japan's advantage. The next step was to put pressure on Chiang by isolating him from foreign support.

Background to the Pacific War

Fighting in China did not weaken Japanese preparations for war on a larger scale. Industry was stimulated by demand for war materials, and soldiers received valuable battlefield experience. In 1937 the Japanese began a secret programme of warship construction, and within four years some navy leaders thought they were well enough equipped to fight any enemy fleet in the Western Pacific.

Japan hoped to make an alliance with Germany or Britain that would put pressure on Chiang and compel him to make concessions. Such an alliance would also strengthen Japan's position against Russia. Most leaders were particularly attracted to the idea of alliance with Germany, who was the obvious enemy of Russia in the west. Plans for an agreement in early 1939 failed because Germany wanted a more general alliance, aimed partly against Britain and America, rather than a simple anti-Russian treaty. Negotiations continued until August 1939 when Germany signed a non-aggression pact with the Soviet Union. The Japanese government was shocked by Germany's action. It was also angry, as it appeared that Tokyo had deliberately been made to look foolish. This resulted in a reaction against Germany that lasted until her dramatic victories in Europe in 1940. When France was defeated, and it seemed that Britain would be forced to surrender, Japan negotiated a Tripartite Pact with Germany and Italy. This was signed in September 1940.

The Tripartite Pact was designed as a defence against those countries its members were not already at war with. Japan also hoped the agreement would lead to better relations with Russia with whom it signed a neutrality agreement in April 1941. The Japanese were also interested in the natural resources of the western powers' South-East Asian colonies. Japan hoped the pact would guarantee that it would take control of the colonies of the defeated European powers. Perhaps more important, Tokyo believed that the pact would help bring about an end to the war in China. Similarly, Tokyo thought Chiang's government would collapse if outside support was cut off, and that America would become more isolated and less likely to intervene in Chinese problems.

Relations with America, which had been poor since the Japanese occupation of Manchuria, continued to deteriorate between 1937 and 1940. At first, American reaction to the situation in China had been limited to disapproval. In fact, the US government generally followed a policy of non-involvement in foreign conflicts. But Japanese actions in China made American opinion more hostile, and these feelings deepened when the Japanese signed the Tripartite Pact with Nazi Germany and Italy. Though America's army was small, her navy was powerful enough to deter Japan from resorting to force without first exhausting all possibility of a diplomatic settlement. This was particularly important as the Japanese cabinet had decided that they had to take advantage of the war in Europe to gain control of the supplies of rubber, oil and other raw materials

GREATEST EXTENT OF JAPAN'S EMPIRE IN WORLD WAR II

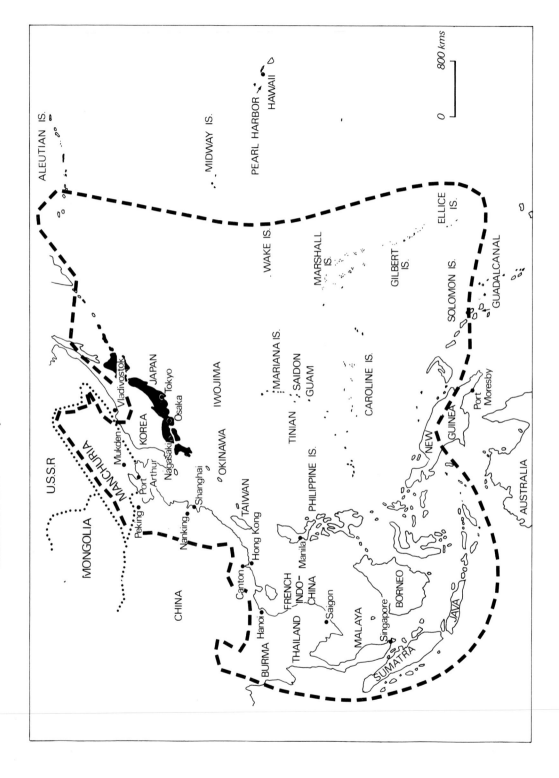

The Greater East Asia Congress, 1943. Representatives from all Japan's occupied territories — China, Thailand, Manchuria, the Philippines, Burma and India — were called to Tokyo to strengthen their 'alliance'. Who is seated centre, front row?

available in Indo-China, Malaya and the Dutch East Indies. America was becoming more closely involved with Britain and was supplying her with arms. There was also a possibility that the US would stop supplying oil to Japan. The Japanese planned to create a 'New Order' in East Asia which would be self-sufficient in natural resources and would not need American oil.

In September 1940 France, which was now occupied by Germany, agreed to allow Japanese troops into north Indo-China to increase pressure on the Chinese by cutting them off from supplies from the south. In July 1941 larger forces occupied the rest of Indo-China, ready for an advance south. Any threat of attack by Russia was removed by the German invasion the month before. The Japanese considered helping Germany, but decided to honour the neutrality agreement with the USSR. Only worries over American reactions prevented a general move south to take over Dutch and British colonies. The Americans believed that their defences in the Pacific were strong enough to resist any attack by Japanese forces, though they did not expect such an attack to take place. They thought that Japan could be controlled by imposing economic sanctions. First, exports of aviation fuel and scrap-iron to Japan were limited by a licence system. This was followed by a more general ban on iron and steel shipments in November 1940. In the following July there was a total ban on exports to Japan and her assets in the US were frozen. This cut Japan's oil imports to a tenth of their previous total, and left the navy with reserves for only two years' operations.

The Japanese leaders were still anxious to avoid war, though the navy was secretly planning and training for attacks on US bases. The Japanese were prepared to withdraw from South Indo-China and from their alliance with Germany. In return, they wanted American assistance to reach a settlement with Chiang Kaishek and help in securing the oil and other raw materials that Japan needed.

At one point, it seemed possible that Prime Minister Konoe might meet with President Roosevelt in Hawaii or Alaska in an attempt to preserve peace, but this did not happen. Konoe resigned and General Tojo took over his post. The Americans delivered a set of ten proposals designed to resolve the situation. Some of these proposals called for Japan's complete withdrawal from China and Indo-China. This created the impression in Japanese minds that America was determined to provoke war. The final decision to launch a Japanese attack was made at an imperial conference on 1 December 1941.

Battleships of the US Pacific Fleet ablaze at Pearl Harbor, 7 December 1941

Pacific War

Just before 8 o'clock in the morning of Sunday 7 December 1941 Japanese planes attacked the naval base of Pearl Harbor in Hawaii. The Americans had intelligence information that an attack was planned, but thought the most likely target was the Philippines. Enemy planes and submarines had been detected but the Americans were still taken by surprise. The attack was a dramatic tactical victory and the American losses in ships, planes and men were very heavy. However, the success of the attack was considerably lessened as Japan failed to sink three American aircraft carriers which were at sea when the raid took place.

Within hours of the Pearl Harbor attack most of the American aircraft based in the Philippines were destroyed on the ground. Other attacks were made on Guam, Wake, Midway and Hong Kong. Altogether 90% of America's air and sea forces in the Pacific area were destroyed or immobilised in the first days of the war. The British warships *Repulse* and *Prince of Wales* were sunk by planes from Japanese aircraft carriers. They had no fighter cover. The importance of naval air power in modern warfare was proved in the first weeks of the Pacific War.

The Japanese army's successes were no less dramatic than those of the navy and air force. Within a few months the Philippines, the Dutch East Indies, Malaya, and most of Burma were under Japanese control. The allied generals underestimated the courage and endurance of the Japanese soldiers. It seemed that no mountains, jungles or rivers were too difficult for them to cross and that no one could defeat them. The capture of the British base of Singapore was expected to take months, but it was completed within ten weeks. Less than 200,000 Japanese troops took part in the advance that extended the Japanese empire almost as far as Australia, and the borders of India.

The American people were shocked by the attack on Pearl Harbor and immediately united in an all-out war effort. Despite the vast resources of the America economy it took time to convert it to full-scale war production. The US counter-attack was also slowed by the decision to defeat Germany first, and then turn the full resources of the Allies against Japan.

General Tojo photographed when Prime Minister

The Japanese advance was halted in New Guinea and at the Battle of the Coral Sea. The tide of war turned against Japan at the naval battle of Midway in June 1942 when four Japanese carriers were sunk by American aircraft. Some of these US planes flew from carriers that escaped the Pearl Harbour attack six months earlier. The American victory at Guadalcanal in the Solomon Islands in February 1943 was the start of a general advance against Japan. The aim of the Allied strategy, known as 'island hopping,' was not to retake all the Japanese-held islands but to concentrate on attacking bases that could be used to dominate wide areas through air power, and for further advances.

The Japanese army units on island bases were often isolated and brought close to starvation. They depended on supplies brought by merchant ships, but these were often sunk by American submarines. Three quarters of the Japanese merchant fleet was sunk by the beginning of 1945. New ships were hurriedly built to replace them, but their quality was often poor. New production was exceeded by the numbers destroyed and the size of the merchant fleet fell steadily. The loss of merchant ships meant that Japan became isolated from its empire and was unable to transport the supplies of raw materials that its industry needed. Japan also fell behind in the development of air power and became short of trained pilots. As a result in 1944 and 1945 suicide tactics were increasingly used, and pilots volunteered to crash-dive into American ships. Hundreds of these suicide attacks were made but less than 3% were successful in hitting Allied ships. The army was equally determined in its resistance to American attempts to capture their island bases. Japanese troops fought to the last man. To take Iwo Jima, a tiny coral island, American forces carried out five weeks of bombardment before the invasion. A month of bitter fighting followed in which all 23,000 Japanese defenders died and 20,000 Americans were killed or wounded. The capture of such small islands as Saipan (in 1944) provided America with bases from which bombers could attack the Japanese mainland.

Young evacuees from Tokyo arriving at their destination

War at Home

The life of ordinary people in Japan was strictly controlled during the war years. In 1938 the National Mobilisation Law limited people's freedom and gave them new duties. In 1941 the Peace Preservation Law was changed so that political prisoners could be held in prison even when they had completed their sentences. Despite these measures the Meiji Constitution was never altered or suspended during the war.

News about the war was mostly limited to official announcements issued by the armed forces. News of defeats, such as that at Midway, were held back from the public and no articles criticising the war, were allowed to appear.

In 1940 the Imperial Rule Assistance Association (IRAA) was formed bringing together the different political parties and the trade unions in an attempt to unite the country behind the war effort. The IRAA used local organisations, such as village associations, to reach ordinary people but its activities were largely confined to propaganda. The Association never suceeded in setting up a one-party state like that in Nazi Germany, and its organisation was generally clumsy. Unlike Germany, Japan's leadership changed as the war situation deteriorated. Even Prime Minister Tojo whom the Allies saw as Japan's equivalent of Hitler, was forced to resign in 1944.

A government planning board was set up to run the economy, set wages and prices, and to organise labour and trade. In 1943 the law was changed to enable women to work more than eleven hours each day, and to allow them to work at night. The two-day minimum rest period for women each month, was also suspended. The economy suffered from shortages of raw materials as the war progressed. By the middle of 1944 supplies of pig iron and coking coal were cut to a third of their pre-war quantities. Deep-sea fishing, which had been an important industry, was rarely carried out in the last year of the war, and fish supplies were reduced to a fifth of their 1941 level. Despite these limitations Japanese industry produced some remarkable technical achievements. These included a submarine that could carry fighter planes and a type of torpedo that was more powerful than anything that was produced by Britain or America. Some of this technical expertise was useful when Japan's industry began to recover after the war.

Rationing began in 1941 with rice, but was soon followed by vegetables, fish and clothing. Twenty per cent of rice had to be imported and as early as 1942 wheat and barley sometimes had to be provided in place of the rice ration. Sweet potatoes became another rice substitute and a thriving black market developed for all the goods that were in short supply. After April 1945 no rice could be brought from Formosa (Taiwan) and the harvest in Japan that year was the lowest since 1909. The daily ration was reduced to less than 1500 calories. This, was not quite starvation level but low enough to affect people's health and ability to work. Illness was another major problem and over 150,000 people died from tuberculosis in each year of the war.

Central Tokyo, August 1945, after a year of bombing

The most dramatic impact of the last years of war on people in Japan's cities was bombing. First, there were attacks on military targets and factories and then fire raids on whole cities. Incendiary bombs were dropped by the thousand and one by one towns and cities were burnt to the ground. Japanese houses were made mainly of wood and so burned easily. In one raid on Tokyo at least 80,000 people were burned to death. To escape this terror, first children and then non-essential adults were moved to the countryside. By the end of the war over 8,000,000 people had been evacuated throughout Japan. American bombing also disrupted railways and factory production. It has been estimated that the damage done to the civilian economy of Japan in the war months of 1945 was greater than that caused by three years of bombing in Germany.

Oil supplies were almost exhausted by 1945 and charcoal, and vegetable oils were used as fuels for motor vehicles. Children and old people were employed in digging up the roots from old pine trees from which small quantities of oil could be extracted. Students had to give up their education to enter the army or work in factories. Food was scarce and prices were rising. Despite these desperate conditions plans were made to fight off the expected Allied invasion. Millions of civilian volunteers were to fight alongside army units and ensure that the invader's casualties were so heavy that they would be prepared to make peace rather than attempt to conquer the entire country.

Asia for the Asians

The Japanese often saw themselves as liberators when they conquered territory that had previously been controlled by the British, Dutch or Americans. They presented themselves as the saviours of the native populations from western colonial rule. In Burma and the Dutch East Indies particularly, they were well received at first. Native governments were set up in some countries and local languages encouraged.

The Japanese gave Burma and the Philipppines 'independence,' though this did not include control of foreign relations and military affairs. Japanese was made the second language in most parts of the empire and their national anthem was sung in public places. In an attempt to replace western colonial governments, the Great East Asia Ministry was established in 1942. It was staffed by civilians and was responsible for foreign relations within the empire. It also encouraged local cultural and religious leaders to visit Japan. In practice, the Japanese army, or navy, controlled local affairs and native governments. The civilians from the Great East Asia Ministry, were treated with little respect by the Japanese armed forces in most occupied areas.

Reactions to the Japanese, and their treatment of their subjects, varied in different parts of the empire. In Thailand the monarchy was allowed to remain and the government allowed a lot of control over its own affairs. Relations with the occupying army were comparatively good and so there was little anti-Japanese feeling. In China, a pro-Japanese puppet government was set up in Nanjing (Nanking) but it had little influence as army commanders preferred to support their own local puppet leaders. China's natural resources were exploited and

Why They Dropped the Atomic Bombs

Whether or not the Allies needed to drop the two atomic bombs on Japan has been argued about since 1945. Here are some points that have come into these arguments.

1. The Allied leaders thought that an invasion of the Japanese mainland would be needed to ensure Japan's unconditional surrender. They thought that such an invasion might result in as many as a million Allied casualties. If an invasion was made, the Japanese were certain to kill thousands of Allied prisoners of war.

2. Japan was already defeated and trying to negotiate peace. The intervention of Russia in the war might, alone, have caused the Japanese to surrender.

3. A demonstration to reveal the power of the bomb could have been tried on an uninhabited Japanese island. Allied leaders thought that this would not have impressed the Japanese enough to bring about a surrender. They also argued that the Japanese would draft prisoners-of-war into target cities if they knew that such attacks were possible.

4. The atomic bombs were weapons, and Allied commanders wanted to test the effects of such weapons on a proper target. The use of the bombs could also act as a warning to Russia, who was seen as a potential enemy of America and Western Europe after the war was over.

5. Though the affects of the bombs were terrible, the knowledge of what they could do has helped prevent such weapons being used since 1945.

thousands of Chinese were sent to Japan to work as forced labour. Koreans were pressed to adopt Japanese names and 370,000 of them were conscripted into the Japanese armed forces or as labourers. In 1942 the Indian National Army (INA) was formed from Indians who lived in Malaya or who were taken prisoner at Singapore. The INA was supposed to help the liberation of India, but did little fighting. In the Philippines the US government had already promised independence and there was generally a pro-American feeling within the population. A good deal of resistance to the occupation developed. Many sugar fields were converted to cotton which was more useful to the Japanese economy. This and other changes produced resistance and by the end of the occupation there were thousands of guerrillas operating against the Japanese army in the Philippines.

The Japanese did not have the time or the resources to develop the different parts of their empire. They had little chance to carry out any major programmes to improve education, transport and agriculture and were reduced to simply exploiting the natural resources of the conquered countries. As some of these became isolated from the Japanese mainland local populations began to suffer greater hardships through shortages. By 1944 it was clear that Japan was losing the war and this led some nationalist groups to turn against the Japanese. In many areas this meant organising guerilla units to fight against the Japanese army.

Many guerilla groups were communist and this factor was important after the war as it gave local communist parties significant influence in many countries in South-East Asia. One of the most important effects of the Pacific war was the post-war independence of Asian colonial territories. It was very difficult for western nations to resume control over their former colonies when the fighting was over, and several countries soon gained independence.

Ending the War

Japan lost the war because it could not match the vast industrial production of the American economy. The Japanese gained their empire with its supplies of raw materials, but they did not have time to link the economies of the conquered countries with their own. They were also unable to defend such a vast area against Allied counter-attack. As early as 1943 some diplomats in Japan began to think that peace should be made. A few leaders already realised that Japan was losing the war but they dared not voice these opinions because they feared army extremists. The capture of Saipan, in July 1944, gave the Americans a base from which they could bomb Japan in earnest. This led to the fall of Tojo and from this time on leaders who were prepared to make peace with the Allies began to gain influence.

In July 1945 the Allied leaders issued the Potsdam Declaration to the Japanese. They were told to surrender unconditionally or face 'prompt and utter destruction.' The future position of the Emperor was not made clear and so the Japanese chose to fight on. What was meant by 'utter destruction' was shown on 6 August 1945 when the first atomic bomb attack was made on Hiroshima. The city had suffered little damage in previous raids but within seconds of the atomic explosion it had almost ceased to exist and thousands were killed by the blast. Many more thousands died during the next few hours in fires and from

A church in ruins 900 metres east-north-east of the hypercentre, Hiroshima. The atomic blast and the fire that followed destroyed 92% of the city's 76,000 buildings.

The Effects of the Hiroshima Attack

The bomb that was dropped from the American B.29 bomber on Hiroshima, on 6 August 1945, exploded almost 600 metres above the city centre. The temperature at 'ground zero,' immediately below the explosion was several thousand degrees and people there were turned into vapour.

The flash of the explosion started fires for up to a mile away and burned the skin of people in the open up to two miles away. About 80,000 people were killed in the explosion, or died soon afterwards from burns and other injuries. In many cases clothing was fused to peoples' skins.

A firestorm followed the flash and shock of the explosion. Two-thirds of all the buildings in the city were destroyed. Among those flattened was the medieval castle which was about three hundred metres from ground zero.

In the weeks that followed the attack, the effects of radiation began to show. Skin peeled and hair fell out. Wounds would not heal. Today breast and thyroid cancer are more common amongst atom bomb survivors than in other Japanese. Yet these survivors have a greater life expectancy than the rest of the population. Only the fittest could have survived the effects of the attack. Survivors hold a 'green card' that entitles them to free medical examination and treatment.

Today, the area around ground zero is preserved as a Peace Park. Close by is the A-bomb dome. It was the Hiroshima Prefectural building for the Promotion of Industry and was the first building in the city to be made of steel and concrete. Its ruin serves as a memorial to the events of 6 August 1945.

The A-Bomb Dome (originally the city's Promotion of Industry building) seen through the memorial of the Hiroshima Peace Park and Museum

their injuries, and they continued to die in the following days from the effects of radiation.

The situation for Japan became even more desperate when the Russians invaded Manchuria early on 9 August. Later that day, a second atomic bomb was dropped on the city of Nagasaki. Some Japanese leaders still wished to fight on but the Emperor called for acceptance of the Allies' terms. On 15 August Emperor Hirohito's recorded speech was broadcast to the nation, informing the people that Japan had accepted the Allies' Potsdam Declaration.

Record of the Emperor's reading of the Surrender Rescript broadcast on 15 August 1945

POINTS TO CONSIDER

1.   Chinese resistance was much greater than Japan expected and it became impossible for Japan to find a satisfactory way to end the war in China.
2.   The Japanese felt that they were forced to advance south to develop a self-sufficient empire because of what they saw as hostile American policies.
3.   The Allies were surprised by the quality and determination of Japanese land, sea and air forces.
4.   The Japanese conquests changed the political situation in the former colonies of the western nations, and some moved rapidly to independence after the war.
5.   The Japanese never expected to totally defeat America. They hoped to carve out an empire that they could successfully defend. In the end they could not match the vast power of the American economy.
6.   By the middle of 1945 Japan was totally defeated but it took atomic bombs and a Russian attack to force her unconditional surrender.

QUESTIONS

(a)   Why did Japan go to war with the Allies in 1941?
(b)   Describe the effects of the war on the countries that Japan conquered.

8 The Countryside

A Japanese village in the 1870s

The Tokugawa Countryside

In the seventeenth century Japan consisted mainly of thousands of small, isolated villages with an economy largely based on the growing and marketing of rice. In general, peasants simply grew enough rice for their own family needs and to pay taxes, plus a small surplus to buy basic commodities. Many peasants, however, could not afford to eat rice and lived instead on a diet of millet and other grains. The countryside fed the cities and paid taxes to the government or to local rulers. Tax was taken as a percentage of the crop grown by the peasants, and on average this amounted to 50%. Levels of prosperity varied considerably because in some areas the land was better or farming know-how was better or both. Generally, the Kyoto region (south-west) was rich and the north-east was poor. This pattern remained until the Second World War.

Living Conditions

Life revolved around the village and few, if any, knew much of the world outside its boundaries. Many villages had been settled for hundreds of years and custom and tradition were very strong. Life in the Japanese countryside was hard and the cultivation of rice was back-breaking work and was very labour-intensive. However, better methods of farming improved living standards in the eighteenth and nineteenth centuries. A good harvest meant a family or village would have enough to eat, and be able to buy extra goods from passing traders or village merchants. A poor harvest might mean shortages until the next season, or even serious food problems, including starvation. Despite the overall growth in prosperity during the Tokugawa period, the margin of survival was often narrow. There were, for instance, severe regional famines in the 1730s, 1780s and 1830s that took many lives.

Changes in Agriculture

Between 1600 and 1720 there were important changes in the Japanese countryside. Agricultural productivity increased, and new crops were introduced, such as cotton, tobacco and cereals, for the developing city centres of Edo (Tokyo) and Osaka. A large-scale trade in rice developed from the countryside

---

DOCUMENT 1 | ### *Peasants, Rebels and Outcastes; the Underside of Modern Japan* *Hane Mikiso (1982)*

Western technology slowly began to filter into the villages. Initially, certain objects astounded and frightened the populace. An item in a newspaper in 1873 reported that a young *geisha* fainted with fright when a customer lit a match; she thought a ghost had appeared. Another account in 1872 related that the peasants of western Japan believed the rumour that telegraph lines were infused with the blood of virgins who had been specially conscripted by the goverment to supply blood for the lines; to avoid a similar fate, young women shaved their eyebrows and blackened their teeth in hopes of passing for married women.

The peasants' reluctance to change their ways also revealed itself in their dogged adherence to the old calendar. One critic protested; 'We have come along thus far with the traditional calendar, and it has caused no trouble to anyone. Why has the government suddenly decided to abolish it? The old system corresponded to the seasons, the weather, and the movement of the tides. One could plan one's work, one's clothing and virtually everything else by it. Since the revision, the New Year and Obon (Buddhist festival) come at crazy times. In the fourth and fifth months, snow and frost are still on the ground....Nothing is the way it should be.'

1. *Is this a primary or secondary source?*
2. *Why was there opposition to the new calendar in the countryside?*
3. *In what other ways did western ideas and technology affect the countryside at this time?*

to the cities. The area of cultivated land was extended by means of drainage and irrigation and improved strains of rice and other crops were developed. By the late eighteenth century the Japanese peasant was the most technically advanced in Asia, and produced more efficiently than many farmers of the developing world today.

The progress of the Tokugawa economy affected the lives of villagers in many ways. The use of money became more widespread and the growth of crops for sale meant that peasants' lives depended more and more on outside factors, such as a rise or fall in the price of rice or silk. After 1600, too, a new class of richer peasants emerged. They were often people who had taken advantage of the new markets provided by growing cities to grow special crops to sell there. In time, many of these richer peasants employed more workers and became influential figures in their villages. They were also responsible for the introduction of some of the new small-scale manufacturing industries such as cotton cloth and rice wine that appeared towards the end of the period.

The Meiji Countryside

Overall, the Meiji restoration brought both benefits and losses to the Japanese peasant. Before 1868 most land in Japan was owned by the shogunate and the *daimyo*, but after that date the new government recognised private ownership of land. The government also encouraged better methods of farming. However, with improved transport and telegraph, central government policies and administration were gradually extended throughout the countryside.

Land Tax

The aim of the new government was to create a strong, centralised administration with a uniform tax system. In 1872 the government removed the ban on the sale of land and conducted a nation-wide land survey. The following year a new land tax was introduced which replaced the traditional payment of tax in rice. Now the peasants had to pay their taxes in cash. This was calculated at 3% of the value of the land cultivated by each individual farmer. This produced many local protests but none was successful. In the first ten years of the Meiji era there were over 200 protests. A number of factors contributed to peasant unrest at this time. Tensions in the villages between rich and poor peasants accounted for many disturbances, but after 1870 many risings were sparked by the government's reform programme; the new land tax, changes in social customs and the ending of the old system of rule by local lords caused widespread unrest. Despite this unsettled start, between 1873 and the 1890s the land tax represented 70-80% of the government's income.

The Countryside and Modernisation

Japan remained largely an agrarian society up to the First World War. In 1868 over 80% of the population lived in the countryside and were engaged in agriculture. The countryside played a vital role in industrialisation for land taxes

DOCUMENT 2   **The Most Exacting Crop in the World**
J. W. Robertson Scott (1922)

One day when I went into the country it happened to be raining hard, but the men and women toiled in the paddies. They were breaking up the flooded clods with a tool resembling the 'pulling fork' used in the West for getting manure from a dung cart. The men and women in the paddies kept off the rain by means of the usual wide straw hats and loose straw mantles, admirable in their way in their combination of lightness and rainproofness....

Planting time arrives in the middle of June or thereabouts. It is illustrative of the exacting ways of rice that not only has it to have a growing place specially fashioned for it, it cannot be sown as cereals are sown. It must be sown in beds and then transplanted. The seed beds have been sown in the latter part of April or the early part of May.... Within about thirty or forty days the seedlings are ready for transplanting.

The rate at which the planters, working in a row across the paddy, set out the seedlings in the mud below the water is remarkable. The first weeding or raking takes place about a fortnight after planting.... Most of the weeding is done simply by thrusting the hand into the mud (and) pulling out the weed. As much of (the work) is done in the hottest time of the year the workers protect themselves by wide-brimmed hats...and by flapping straw cloaks or by bundles of straw fastened on their backs.

1. *Why is growing rice such a time-consuming business?*
2. *What is significant about the fact that men and women worked together in the rice fields?*
3. *Would you be likely to see such a scene in the countryside today?*

were used to pay for new factories. The export of raw materials and the profits made from agriculture were also used to support the development of industry, with government help. Agricultural efficiency increased and managed to keep pace with the increase in population. The growth of productivity occurred largely as a result of a continuation of the kinds of developments that had taken place during the Tokugawa era: improved irrigation, land reclamation, use of fertilisers, new crops and improved crop strains. Furthermore, the growth of industrial towns provided new markets for agricultural produce.

Although the government taxed the countryside to help provide the funds to develop industry, it also brought progress in many areas. The government encouraged the development of new technology, especially in silk. As a result of government encouragement silk production in Japan increased 12 times during the Meiji period. The government sent agricultural experts abroad to study foreign methods, agricultural colleges were set up and technical advice and information were passed on to villagers by government instructors. New and improved crops were introduced and the area of land under cultivation increased. In particular, the northern island of Hokkaido was opened up to American-style agriculture and dairy farming. Not all government experiments were successful, although there was much technical progress in the Japanese countryside. All of these improvements took place without altering the basic pattern of farming villages. The size of plots remained very small and there was little opportunity to introduce mechanisation.

Modernisation brought other changes to the villages of Japan. The Education Act of 1872 made primary education compulsory, and although at first there was a high level of absenteeism, by the end of the century nearly 100% of rural children were attending school. By 1900, many villages were linked to the towns and cities by road and railway. However, many basic facilities such as gas and electricity which were common in Japanese cities did not appear in the countryside until after the First World War.

Living Conditions

Peasant houses were usually small and thatched with straw. A number of improvements were seen after 1868 as tiles were used for roofing and coarse straw matting was replaced by finely woven *tatami* mats. Translucent paper and glass started to be used for windows and dividing doors. As in European villages, sanitation facilities were primitive and human waste was used as fertiliser. Kerosene lamps were used to light peasant homes during the Meiji period, gradually replacing the wax candles and vegetable oil lamps used previously. In areas with relatively mild winters people kept warm in the winter by sitting around a charcoal-burning brazier. In northern areas where the winters were more severe, some houses had a hearth built in or near the kitchen, and the family would spend winter nights huddling round it.

Unlike many city-dwellers, the food eaten by the majority of villagers was generally of rather low quality — the typical diet being made up largely of carbohydrates; a survey at the end of the Meiji period showed that about two-thirds of the money spent by peasant families on food went on rice while poor peasants often made do with millet, barley or yams. Meat was virtually unknown in most village households at this time. Some peasants supplemented their diet with small amounts of fish, but the varieties of fruit and vegetables being grown in the countryside after 1868 were largely for the urban market.

Many peasants lived in relatively unhealthy conditions and diseases such as cholera, typhoid, small-pox and dysentery took considerable numbers of lives in the rural areas until well into the twentieth century. Epidemics of these diseases were not finally brought under control until after 1945. The poor diet of the Japanese peasant was reflected in the high incidence of tuberculosis and beri beri, while infant mortality remained high and life expectancy relatively low until after 1945 when a remarkable transformation in the nation's health took place. Medical facilities in the countryside were usually basic and the more remote villages often had no access to a doctor. Medical care was more widely available in villages that were closer to towns and cities, though many peasants often could not afford the fees of the local doctor.

Tenants and Landlords

As the nineteenth century progressed more and more peasants were forced to sell their land and become tenants paying rent to landlords. Most tenants paid rent in kind, and on average, the amount was about half their crop. Ownership of land passed into fewer hands; in 1872 about 20% of peasants were tenants, by the end of the Meiji period this had risen to almost 50%. This pattern of tenancy remained fairly constant until 1945.

The social and economic changes of the Tokugawa period had produced a new landlord class whose power and influence increased in the years after 1868. Until the 1920s most landlords lived in villages and many were themselves farmers. Most landlord holdings were relatively small, and the phenomenon of large estates found in Europe and other Asian countries did not really exist in Japan. The landlords played a key role in the social and political life of the villages. Some historians have viewed the landlords unfavourably, but they did play an important part in introducing new techniques and crops to the countryside. They also gave help in setting up village schools and, occasionally, medical services. On the other hand, landlords were often unwilling to carry out reforms that would threaten their control over village affairs. However, when landlords moved to live in towns they had less detailed control of village life.

Silk

The rural economy made a significant contribution to developing Japan's early industries and productivity kept pace with the growing population. However, Japanese agriculture had a number of problems. The growth of tenancy and the gap between rich and poor peasants in the villages were two serious problems. The greatest weakness of Japanese agriculture, after about 1900, was its reliance on a single product, silk, for added income — particularly as the price of silk depended on conditions overseas. This was made worse by the fact that nearly three-quarters of all Japanese silk products were sold to a single market — the United States.

The Taisho Countryside

The Japanese population increased significantly after 1868 but the proportion living in the countryside dropped steadily from that time as more and more people migrated to the new job opportunities of the 'new Japan' which were virtually all to be found in the towns and cities. However by 1914 the rural population was still about 16 million, and even as late as 1940 there were over 14 million people working in agriculture and fishing.

During the Taisho period (1912-1926) rice remained the chief food crop grown by the peasants and accounted for well over 50% of arable land. Rice imports from Japan's colonies, Korea and Taiwan, increased and by the end of the 1920s Japan relied on these imports to meet the growing food demands of her cities. The cities also stimulated the demand for new types of food, and after 1914 the range of fruit and vegetables grown in the countryside increased considerably.

The main technical change during this period was the use of fertilisers. This

DOCUMENT 3   **The women of Suye Mura**   (*Rural living conditions, 1935*)
Robert J. Smith and Ella Lury Wiswell (1982)

The kitchen was a lean-to with a dirt floor and a built-in wood-burning stove. There was no running water and no heat. Water had to be brought from the nearby well in buckets suspended from a yoke over the shoulder. Bath water heated to what seemed almost the boiling point proved a blessing in the winter months, but keeping warm otherwise was very difficult and we just about grew into our woollen underwear. The winter in Suye was mild compared to many other parts of Japan, but sliding paper doors do not keep out the cold air and charcoal braziers do not provide much heat. In the morning, it was always a trial to abandon… warm robes and get into our clothes in a cold, unheated room. In the winter everybody in the village suffered from chilblains. In the summer there were the heat, mosquitoes, and the pervasive smell of 'night soil' fertiliser used on the rice fields a few paces away from the back of our houses. Like everyone else, we slept on the floor under a huge mosquito net suspended from the ceiling. One night, to my great consternation, I found a field mouse inside the netting.

1. What does the passage tell you about life in a pre-war Japanese village?
2. What changes did peasants experience in the 1930s; (a) in income (b) in living conditions?

was partly encouraged by the growth of the Japanese chemical industry which was now able to supply farmers with a wide variety of products. In addition, there were important improvements to living conditions in the countryside; in particular, electricity started to appear in villages in the 1920s. Overall, however, the gap between the cities and the countryside widened in the period after the First World War. A fall in the price of rice after 1918 affected some peasant incomes and led in the mid 1920s to government subsidies to support the price. The subsidy, however, could not stop the price of rice from falling steadily from 1927 onwards marking the beginning of what was to be almost ten years of hardship in some areas — despite the fact that between 1927 and 1930 the Japanese peasant farmer harvested four consecutive bumper crops. However, cheap imports from Korea and Taiwan kept prices low and few Japanese farmers gained much benefit.

Agrarian Problems

After the First World War the growth of Japanese cities and the economic depression in the countryside had two important results. Firstly, many landlords no longer found it desirable to live in the country, and decided to move to the cities. In their place they left agents to collect their rents from the tenants, and rent-collecting became an impersonal matter. Secondly, the peasants began to organise themselves into tenant unions. Tenant associations had appeared as early as the 1870s, but it was the increasing confidence of many farmers that often stimulated growth. The emergence of the tenant unions was similar to the trade union movement in industry and the cities. The 1920s witnessed a significant rise in disputes between landlords and tenants; in 1918 there were nearly 300 disputes, and by 1921 almost 1700. The result of this was the establishment of the Japan Peasants' Union in 1922. This campaigned for a reform to enable tenants to buy their farms. It also sought a minimum wage and laws to protect tenants against landlords. Although there were 365,000 members of tenant unions by 1927, the movement was never able to achieve a nation-wide influence, and after that time membership declined as a result of divisions within the leadership and police pressure.

Rural women in work clothes in the 1930s

Depression and War

Parts of the Japanese countryside had been suffering from economic difficulties throughout most of the 1920s, and the effects of the world depression of the 1930s were very severe. Almost overnight, this destroyed the peasants' main source of extra income: silk. There had been a three-fold increase in silk production between 1914 and 1929 and 40% of all farming families had silk as an extra source of work and income.

In 1929-1930 the American market for silk collapsed and the effects of this hit Japan at almost the same time as the dramatic fall in the price of rice. As a result, some families in north-eastern Japan were pushed into worsening conditions especially when a bad harvest hit the northern areas in 1934. In some parts, it was the farmers' confidence, and in other cases it was distress which increased discontent and hostile feelings towards politicians and large companies who were blamed for these difficulties. The army drew many of its soldiers from the countryside, and news of the situation there helped to stimulate nationalism and hostility to the political parties. Some historians have argued that rural distress was an important cause of extreme nationalism in Japanese politics in the 1930s. Certainly, it encouraged some peasants to emigrate to Manchuria.

The situation in certain areas of the countryside was serious until the mid 1930s when the price of rice began to rise again. The price of raw silk, however, remained low and in 1936 was still half of what it had been in 1929. This contributed to a large-scale migration of peasants to the cities where they found jobs in industry. Many others were conscripted into the armed forces.

Woman on her way to the fields with traditional farm implements in the 1930s

The Countryside during the War

After 1937 the need for food was so great that war-time regulations were introduced. These brought some benefits to the peasantry. The government established tight control over the economy and in the countryside an official system for settling tenant-landlord disputes was introduced. The power of landlords was limited and farm rents and land prices were frozen. These measures aimed to increase production and led to an improvement in the incomes and conditions of the peasants. The government paid a special high price for rice marketed by peasants who owned and worked their own land. A quota system was established for crops which were planted on government orders and there was help with seed and fertilisers. However, as the war progressed, the countryside was forced to send many recruits to the army and war industries. It also had to provide food and shelter for the growing number of refugees from bombed cities. However, in the last months of the war the food shortage enabled peasants to obtain very high prices for food sold illegally.

The Post-war Countryside

Land Reform

Japan was devastated by the end of the war, and a priority of the government and the Occupation authorities was to ensure that adequate rice supplies reached the ruined cities. It was vital to keep prices low, and therefore it was considered necessary to reduce farmers' rents. In December 1945, the government introduced a reform to help tenants buy land but the Americans thought it inadequate, and they urged a much more radical land reform in 1946. The Americans believed that the poverty of Japanese peasants and the power of rural landlords had been important causes of Japanese militarism in the 1930s. The land reform aimed to end poverty by converting tenants into land-owning farmers and by eliminating the landlord class. The Americans also feared the possibility of peasant rebellions. As a result, landlords had to sell all their land in excess of a small holding. Land holdings were restricted to no more than 3 hectares per family, plus 1 hectare for rent. These amounts were greater in Hokkaido where there was more land available. Land reform was complex as it required changes in the land rights of almost 6 million peasant families. This wholesale transfer of property was largely completed by 1949 and the Japanese landlord class almost disappeared. The level of tenancy, almost 50% in 1945, dropped to about 8% by the end of the 1940s.

Land reform was the biggest and most successful of the Occupation reforms;

Women planting out rice seedlings by hand in the spring

Preparing a rice field in the early post-war years; (right) a rural scene in the 1970s. What evidence of the 'economic miracle' do you see here?

it ended the problems of rural poverty and tenancy, and paved the way for the prosperity of the 1960s. However, there were a number of serious problems in the rural areas until the 1950s. The last years of the war and the first years of peace saw a large migration from the cities to the relative security of the countryside, and until the 1950s many evacuees remained on the land rather

DOCUMENT 4

Shinohata; a portrait of a Japanese village
Ronald Dore (1978)

In the last twenty years, and especially the last ten, however, the pace of mechanisation has been faster than ever before. Every house now has its two-wheeled multi-purpose tiller to do all the operations for field preparation in a quarter of the time it used to take with an ox. Simple reaper-binder machines have taken the back-breaking labour out of harvesting, though experiments with small-scale combine harvesters have not been successful...., and the sheaves still have to be dried on racks and threshed much as they were twenty years ago. Early weeding of rice fields, groping among the plants with one's fingers, is now an archaic practice, replaced by liberal use of herbicide.... The most spectacular innovation is the rice planter. These smart, brightly painted machines are certainly ingenious. They are loaded with a pack of seedlings grown in special trays and move under their own power across the fields, with a couple of high-speed arms snatching three or four seedlings at a time and embedding them at just the right depth in the mud in rows as straight as the guiding hand of the operator can steer the machine.

1. Read Document 2 again; what are the differences in the growing of rice in 1922 and in 1978?
2. Why is life in the countryside so much easier now than in the pre-war period?
3. 'Experiments with small-scale combine harvesters have not been successful.' Can you suggest any reasons for this?

than return to the hungry cities. There was also the problem of almost 6 million soldiers and colonists returning home from China, Korea and South-East Asia. The majority of those returning settled in the countryside. However, as the Japanese economy began to develop in the 1950s most of these problems disappeared.

Changes in the Countryside after Land Reform

Following the land reforms, Japanese agricultural efficiency increased almost everywhere. The reforms coincided with important developments in agricultural science such as improved fertilisers, pesticides, seeds and cultivation methods. As the Japanese economy began to grow in the mid 1950s a large-scale mechanisation of agriculture started. Small tractors, which were virtually unknown before that time, began to appear and were seen everywhere. Agricultural cooperatives became outlets for the sale of a growing variety of products, and the government helped with technical information and aid. Together, cooperatives negotiated with the government to obtain subsidies especially subsidies for rice farmers. From the late 1950s Japanese agriculture became more varied and was soon producing a wide variety of fruit and vegetables, dairy produce and poultry which reflected the rapid growth of post-war cities. Land reclamation projects and the development of upland areas also contributed to the prosperity of the rural areas. Even the most remote regions were drawn into modern life with radio and television, and improved road and rail communications. The living standards of many peasants had been rising since the beginning of the war, but from the 1950s onwards improvements were experienced all over Japan. The prosperity of the countryside has not only happened as a result of increased agricultural efficiency, but largely as a consequence of Japan's 'industrial miracle.' The boom in the economy in the 1960s and 1970s has benefitted the countryside by providing a wide range of

Paddy fields in Hokkaido. How is this scene different from elsewhere in Japan?

opportunities for great numbers of people living in the rural areas to make a living in non-agricultural work.

The Countryside Today

Since 1955 there has been a dramatic shift in the population balance in Japan as an increasing number of people have left the land to live and work in the cities. In 1955 about 15 million people were engaged in agriculture, but by 1983 this figure had fallen below 4 million. The majority of today's farmers are elderly, and many of these are women. Most farming families now rely to a large extent on non-agricultural income and many are only engaged in part-time farming. Before the Second World War 20% of peasant income came from non-agricultural work; by the late 1970s it was over 60%. This trend has been stimulated by the spread of industry to the countryside and improved communications.

Modern automatic rice-seedling planter. What effect has such technology had on the development of farm life in modern Japan?

Although incomes in the country are less than those in the cities, most rural families have all the modern conveniences, such as cars, stereos, refrigerators, colour television and so on. Houses are often bigger and better in the countryside. In politics, rural Japan exercises an influence out of all proportion to its size, as the majority of small farmers vote for the conservative party. Since 1949, the ruling conservative parties have ensured that the farmers are paid a high price for their products. This system of agricultural subsidies has kept local food prices high, and the government has supported farmers by controlling some foreign imports.

In the 1980s, the Japanese countryside faces problems which are similar to those in the EEC. The amount of farm land is shrinking as industry and housing continue to spread out. Despite this, Japan still produces too much rice and sometimes uses part of the surplus for famine relief in Third World countries.

DOCUMENT 5   *Annual report on agriculture 1983*   Ministry of Agriculture,
Forestry and Fisheries (1984) (Excerpts)

The population flow from rural to urban areas has slowed down in recent years;
preference for settling in rural areas is becoming stronger than ever before. One
of the reasons for this trend is that people today have diverse values and have the
strong desire to improve their lives qualitatively by pursuing something to live for
or spiritual contentment.

Today, increasing numbers of non-farming households exist in farming
communities. Mainly on the outskirts of large cities, the farming communities are
becoming the basis of life for many non-farming households.

The rapid ageing of the farming population has created various problems, such
as excessive work for the aged, health concerns and the deterioration in productivity
and the use of land resources.

Japanese agriculture today faces a host of problems, including the over-supply
of farm products, the slow-down in the increase of income from agriculture, the
ageing labour force, and the severe employment situation. There are also growing
demands for more efficient management and the opening of the market for foreign
farm products.

Slow growth will take root in Japan's economy and society in the future...The
farming community will assume greater responsibility for supplying food to the
nation on a stable basis. At the same time, it will play a greater role in serving as
a place for working and living, as well as providing urban dwellers with a place for
outdoor recreation.

*1. What does the government consider the main problems in the Japanese countryside
today?*
*2. What is the source of this document? How useful is it as a means of understanding
the situation in the Japanese countryside today?*
3. In what ways do you think the countryside will change in the next decade?

*The much improved quality of life of the average small Japanese farming family is evident
throughout the countryside. Note the proximity of the paddy field to the house. What links with
the past can be seen in this photograph?*

POINTS TO CONSIDER

1.   In the Tokugawa period Japan was largely a rice-growing peasant economy. Changes during the period saw the emergence of landlords and the growth of commercial agriculture. A pattern of small farm units emerged.

2.   The Meiji Land Tax was used to fund industrialisation. Although peasants gained some benefits from the Meiji reforms, tenancy rose to nearly 50%. Living conditions in the countryside were hard, food was often poor.

3.   Modernisation brought schools to the villages and growing contact with the outside world in the form of roads and railways. Government instructors gave advice to the farmers on new crops and methods of farming.

4.   In the 1920s many landlords left the countryside and settled in cities. Disputes between tenants and landlords increased and tenant unions were established. The world Depression of the 1930s caused severe hardship in some areas as the price of silk collapsed. Rural distress helped to push politics to the right, but conditions did improve slightly as a result of war-time policies.

5.   Land reform in 1946 transferred land from landlords to tenants at low prices. From the late 1950s Japanese farmers began to experience growing prosperity as the Japanese 'economic miracle' got underway. Mechanisation of agriculture began. A close relationship was forged between the farmers and the conservative parties.

6.   Since 1955 many people have left the land for the cities. Today, Japanese agriculture is mainly in the hands of the elderly, many of them women. Non-agricultural employment makes a significant contribution to rural incomes. Japanese farmers face similar problems of over-production as do farmers in Europe and the USA, although for Japan over-production is confined largely to rice while wheat and soybeans have to be imported.

QUESTIONS

(a)   What contribution did the countryside make to early industrialisation?

(b)   How successful was Land Reform in solving the problems of Japanese agriculture?

Occupation

Japanese surrender documents are signed on board USS Missouri, *anchored in Tokyo Bay, 2 September 1945*

Facing Defeat

When the first American troops landed in Japan at the end of August 1945 they were prepared for resistance. They had expected at least half a million casualties from an armed invasion of Japan. Their experiences in Okinawa led them to expect opposition from rebellious army units. In fact, a few extremists blew themselves up in a Tokyo park but otherwise there was little trouble. The Japanese people were in a state of shock. They were dazed by their defeat and at the same time there was a sense of relief. It was the Emperor who had ordered them to lay down their weapons and this provided the only acceptable excuse for surrender. They had fought in his name and now they had stopped fighting because he had asked them to do so.

At first, most Japanese people stayed out of sight in their homes. In some areas women fled to hide in the mountains. It was the children, tempted by chocolate and chewing gum, who were often the first to make friends with the looting. American soldiers had been ordered to be on their best behaviour and were allowed to make friends with the Japanese. In fact the American soldiers had one of the warmest receptions of any army that ever took control of a foreign country in recorded history. It was not long before Americans, and things American, were popular with nearly all Japanese.

The reaction of the Japanese to the occupying forces is partly explained by the conditions in Japan at the end of 1945. Nearly two million soldiers and civilians had been killed in the war. Many of Japan's cities had been almost totally destroyed. As many as five million homes had been burned by American incendiary bombs or pulled down to make fire breaks. There were severe food shortages everywhere and in some cases whole communities were close to starvation. Many people did not work for money, instead they were given their wages in the form of food. Thousands of people in the cities took their family possessions into the countryside to exchange them for rice.

Prior to the arrival of the Occupation forces, former Japanese soldiers erect street signs in English in central Tokyo

Making a Democracy

The meeting of Allied leaders at Potsdam in July 1945 decided the future of Japan in general terms. They wanted Japan turned into a peaceful democracy. It was left to the Supreme Commander for the Allied Powers (SCAP) to put the ideas of the Potsdam Declaration into effect. SCAP was General Douglas MacArthur, but the initials came to stand for the entire administration of the occupation forces.

The success of the Occupation was partly due to MacArthur's own approach and personality. At the beginning, he worked a seven-day week and rarely took any time off. He set up his headquarters in the Dai Ichi building (formerly the premises of an insurance company) opposite the imperial palace. He lived at the American Embassy and drove to work every day at the same time. MacArthur remained aloof in a way that impressed the Japanese people. He received a thousand letters a month from Japanese asking for advice on ordinary matters.

Emperor Hirohito meets General Douglas MacArthur on 27 September 1945

Such was his confidence that he refused the services of a bodyguard all the time he was in Japan. MacArthur was not concerned with punishing the Japanese for their actions in the war. As he put it, 'SCAP is not concerned with how to keep Japan down, but how to get her on her feet again.'

At first SCAP was only responsible to the American government. This authority was later given up to the Far Eastern Commission in Washington. However, its decisions had to be transmitted through the American government. In practice the system was ineffective. SCAP was usually left to carry on its work and often the Far Eastern Commission could only approve measures that had already gone into effect.

SCAP did not have to work with the same problems that the occupation forces faced in Germany. Washington had managed to resist Russian calls for a division of the country into zones controlled by different Allied powers. Japan was isolated and SCAP could control who came into the country and could force people to leave.

Early Problems

The task that faced SCAP was still enormous. The country was on the verge of starvation: 3,500,000 tons of food had to be brought in from stores that had been built up ready for the invasion. Most of the urban population was vaccinated against smallpox and tuberculosis and over three million Japanese soldiers and civilians had to be brought back to Japan from their lost overseas territories.

Having dealt with the most pressing problems, SCAP then had to put into effect the policies outlined in the Potsdam Declaration. America had been preparing for the occupation of Japan from as early as 1943. Despite this there were few who were experts on Japanese affairs and fewer still fluent in the language. Japanese who had been born in America, called Nisei, were relied upon heavily. Often the Nisei had an understanding of Japanese society that was scarcely more informed than that of SCAP's officials.

An example of this lack of detailed intelligence was the reaction to the Kokuryukai or 'Black Dragon Society'. The name of the society had often been used in newspapers before the war. It actually referred to the Black Dragon River, the Amur, which separates Manchuria from Siberia. By 1945 this group was no longer of any importance. American orders for its dissolution were swift but unnecessary.

The Americans were also short of information when it came to dealing with other organisations. Anyone who could have been involved in helping to start the war was liable to be purged. In practice this meant that a man who had a particular job during the war might be purged. No account was taken of his individual actions, it was enough that he had held a particular post. Over 200,000 people were purged. Most of them were officers in the armed forces, politicians or teachers.

Women queuing up for rice in the suburbs of Tokyo in 1946

Some Japanese were treated as war criminals. Many were accused of individual acts of cruelty. Over 800 were executed. Seven of these were accused of planning the war and were sentenced after a trial in Tokyo that lasted over two years.

Many outside observers thought that the Emperor should have been treated as one of the 'Class A' war criminals, as those accused of starting the war were called. The Emperor even left his palace to meet with MacArthur and to offer himself as solely responsible for the war and his people's actions. MacArthur and the US government wisely decided to ensure that the Emperor did not have to face trial. They also decided to allow him to keep his position, though his powers were altered. MacArthur was sure that SCAP's ability to control the country would be threatened if the Emperor was removed from office. He was even more certain of trouble if the Emperor was put on trial.

Showa

The word, meaning 'enlightened peace,' is the reign name of the present Emperor of Japan, Hirohito. The name was chosen when he was enthroned in 1926. Though the western calendar is often used in Japan there is also a widely-used Japanese system of dating which refers to the reign name. This means that 1986 would be expressed as the 61st year of Showa, or Showa 61.

Hirohito was born on 29 April 1901. He was the eldest of three sons but was a small weak child. In April 1908 his formal education began in a special class that was formed for him at the Peers School, the most exclusive school in Japan. Twelve boys, including two princely cousins, shared his lessons. Among the subjects he studied were geography, calligraphy, singing, gymnastics and science. He became particularly interested in marine biology and has published many books on the subject.

When he was fourteen his father was enthroned as Emperor. In 1921, as Crown Prince, he made the first trip abroad of any heir to the throne. He visited Britain, France, Italy and Holland. During this six-month tour he talked to several European leaders including Pope Benedict XV.

During his reign Emperor Taisho showed signs of madness and Hirohito acted as regent after his return from Europe until his father's death in December 1926. At the beginning of 1924 he married Princess Kuni, now Empress Nagako, and their son, Akihito, the present Crown Prince, was born in 1933.

Until the end of the last war the Emperor was treated with great reverence by all Japanese. This attitude of deep respect, far greater than that shown to any western monarch, made the position of Emperor almost 'god-like,' though he was not regarded as a god in the western sense. With Japan's defeat in 1945 the Emperor took on a role that was less distant from the people. School-children no longer had to bow to the Emperor's portrait. The Emperor began to make public speeches and meet ordinary people.

The Constitution states that the Emperor is the symbol of the State and of the unity of the people. He has no powers related to government. He appoints Prime Ministers, but these are first chosen by the Diet. He also performs other duties with the advice and approval of the government.

A New Constitution

The Emperor made a New Year's radio broadcast in 1946. He renounced his so-called divinity. The Emperor had not been thought of as a god in the western sense. He had been regarded with awe by the Japanese and was thought to live on a different level from his people. Now he began to tour the country. He was seen inspecting farms and talking openly with ordinary people. Japanese feelings of awe towards the Emperor were replaced by respect and affection.

The Potsdam Declaration had called for freedom of speech, thought, religion and fundamental human rights in Japan. A new Constitution was thought to be needed to ensure that these ideals were brought about. SCAP had soon decided that, despite its huge staff, it would work through the existing Japanese governmental systems. It hoped that the Japanese would be able to draft their own new Constitution and revive democracy themselves. In practice, Japanese officials were slow to respond to SCAP's call for action and when they presented draft changes for SCAP's approval they did not go nearly far enough towards bringing democracy to the country.

MacArthur directed his staff to produce their own version of a Constitution which could be submitted to the Japanese government. Like most SCAP solutions to problems, it was largely American in nature, rather than Japanese. However, the Japanese were allowed to make some changes to American proposals and the new Constitution was reluctantly accepted by the Japanese government and was announced in time for the 1947 elections.

A large section of the Constitution was devoted to the position of the Emperor. He was to be 'the symbol of the state and of the unity of the people.' The state was banned from religious activity and education. State Shinto, the religion that had supported the ideals of an aggressive Japan, had already been abolished by SCAP. Most important and acceptable to the majority of Japanese was Article 9 of the Constitution. It said that 'the Japanese people forever renounce war as a sovereign right of the nation.' It also forbade Japan having any armed forces.

The Constitution called for two houses in the Diet. The House of Councillors was to have 250 members; half of these were to be elected every three years. Over half of them represented Japan's 47 prefectures. The rest were to be chosen by national elections.

More power was given to the other section of the Diet which was called the House of Representatives. It had 467 members. All laws could, eventually, be passed by the House of Representatives alone if there was a large enough majority. They were also responsible for the election of the Prime Minister who had to be a member of the Diet, as did at least half the cabinet.

Politics

The political parties that had existed in Japan before the war sprang up again under new names. The three main parties were the Liberals, Progressives and Social Democrats. There were also many small local parties involved in the elections of April 1946. The electorate had been increased by lowering the voting age and allowing women to vote for the first time.

By the 1947 election the Progressive party had disappeared and had been replaced by the Democratic Party. Most of the smaller parties had been absorbed into one or other of the main parties. After the elections the Democrats and Social Democrats formed a coalition government. It managed to pass several reforms but proved unworkable and was forced to resign.

The Liberals replaced the coalition in power, and in January 1949 won a clear majority in the Diet. Their leader, Yoshida Shigeru, became Prime Minister five times. He was conservative and was acceptable to SCAP. (He had been arrested in March 1945 after calling for peace.) Yoshida had an approach which was blunt and direct for a Japanese. He spoke good English and had been ambassador to Britain before the war. At times, he stood up to SCAP and managed to moderate some of its demands.

Communists and Trade Unions

The communists gained increasing support after the war. A few had been released from prison when the Americans arrived in 1945. Others had been indoctrinated as prisoners of the Chinese Red Army. The communists raced with the Social Democrats to control the trade unions that were created after the war and in the 1949 elections managed to gain 35 seats. After this their influence declined. The communists lost further support when there were Russian calls to put the Emperor on trial and Stalin decided to keep thousands of Japanese prisoners as slave labour.

SCAP believed that trade unions were important to the development of democracy in Japan. The Trade Union Act, Labour Relations Act and Labour Standards Act, all passed by the end of 1947, improved workers conditions and allowed them the right to strike. By 1949 there were over thirty thousand trade unions with nearly seven million members. Many Japanese companies developed their own trade unions and these often suffered less from communist-inspired disruption and strikes.

SCAP stopped a general strike in 1947 on the grounds that it would harm the economy. Later, civil servants and local government employees were banned from striking. This was part of a move against the acts of communist agitation. Purges were made of communist supporters in 1949 and a Trade Union Act in the same year restricted political activity within unions.

The Americans' change of attitude towards trade unions was partly due to the defeat of the nationalists in China in 1949. Relations with Russia had deteriorated and the importance of Japan was made clear when South Korea was nearly lost after an invasion from the communist North. As early as 1947 MacArthur had suggested that Japan had achieved enough democracy to manage her own affairs. The Americans increasingly realised that they needed a willing ally in Asia as well as a strategic base.

Other Reforms

Moves against the *zaibatsu* (the huge Japanese corporations) were eventually dropped. Originally, the Americans had felt that the *zaibatsu* would hinder the move towards democracy in Japan. The Deconcentration Act of 1946 broke Mitsui and Mitsubishi up into over three hundred separate firms. However, a total of only nine companies were affected out of the 1200 that SCAP had originally listed for investigation. By 1948 America had begun to realise that Japan's large pre-war companies should be allowed to continue in order to speed Japan's economic recovery.

Perhaps the most important reform that was passed during the Occupation was land reform. In 1946 MacArthur rejected the Diet's own ideas of land reform and forced them to accept a plan suggested by the Australian representative in Japan. Before the war much of the land was owned by absentee landlords. The Owner Farmer Establishment Law forced these landlords to sell most of their land at pre-war prices. The peasants were then allowed to buy the land they

Yoshida Shigeru

Yoshida was born in Shikoku in September 1878. In 1880 he was adopted into the family of a wealthy merchant. He studied at Tokyo University and then went to work in the Foreign Ministry. In 1909 his marriage to the daughter of the Lord Privy Seal helped his career, and later he became Consul-General in Shenyang (Mukden) in Manchuria. In 1928 he was a member of the cabinet of Prime Minister Tanaka. Two years later he was appointed to be Japan's ambassador to Rome. Later he was posted to England.

Yoshida spoke out against the growing power of the army in politics and was imprisoned during the war. He was brought into the government after Japan's surrender and was appointed Prime Minister when the president of the Liberal Party was purged by SCAP. He remained in office for a year, from May 1946, and was again Prime Minister between October 1948 and December 1954.

Yoshida negotiated and signed the Peace Treaty and Security Treaty with America in 1951. After this his popularity declined and his party lost seats in the Diet. In 1954 there were further problems when there was a scandal over shipbuilding contracts and an unpopular economic policy. Pressure from within the Liberal Party forced him to retire in December. He continued to be an influence in politics until his death in 1967.

cultivated on easy terms and with inflated 1946 currency. As a result, 90% of the country's farmers owned their own land. This encouraged increased production and helped prevent the communists from winning support in country areas.

Not all SCAP's reforms were so successful. There had been a move to decentralise government to some extent. The Home Ministry was abolished. More importance was given to the prefectures. This included responsibility for local police forces. It was thought that this would help to encourage democracy. In the confused situation immediately after the war the police lacked the

Yoshida Shigeru

organisation to tackle widespread crime. Later, the police were reorganised on a national basis and a National Police Reserve was created during the Korean war which was later expanded into the National Self-Defence Force. The creation of this force was unpopular with the Japanese as it contradicted the spirit of their constitution. It also absorbed valuable funds which were needed for Japan's economic recovery.

Education was an early target for SCAP reform. Schools were seen as one of the main areas where Japanese had been encouraged to adopt an aggressive attitude. Pupils had learned to revere the Emperor and bow to his portrait.

In 1946 a team of American educationalists toured the country. Their recommendations formed the basis of the 1947 Fundamental Law of Education and the 1948 School Education Act. Some teachers were purged. School books were destroyed and new courses established. At first there were too few teachers and insufficient resources, but gradually a coherent education system developed. The number of universities was increased to 200. This allowed for at least one university in each prefecture, just as there was one in every state in America.

End of the Occupation

In 1951 the Americans began moves to end the Occupation. In September a Peace Treaty was signed in San Francisco. On the same day a Security Treaty was signed between America and Japan. On the basis of this American troops continued to be stationed in Japan. On 28 April 1952 the Occupation of the main islands of Japan formally ended but US troops remained.

The American Occupation had been a benevolent one. There had been far-reaching reforms that were largely successful. There were several factors that helped the recovery of Japan: the realistic attitudes of MacArthur and the Emperor, the hard work of officials and men like Yoshida, and American food and money in the first years of the Occupation. Also important were trade agreements and the provision of equipment when America recognised the need for an ally in the North Pacific. A considerable boost to the economy followed from American spending during the Korean war. Finally, the fact that Japanese workers and managers were determined to restore national prestige aided recovery.

POINTS TO CONSIDER

1.   Japan was in chaos in 1945. Cities were destroyed, there were food shortages and industry and transport were disrupted.
2.   MacArthur's own personality and approach was a factor in making the Occupation acceptable to the Japanese.
3.   The new constitution could not have developed without American intervention, but it became very much accepted by the Japanese people.
4.   The change in relations with Russia and China made Japan an ally rather than a conquered country.
5.   The cold war helped to persuade the Americans to give up their plans to break up all the zaibatsu. This made the recovery of Japan's industries easier.
6.   The Korean war helped the economic recovery of Japan by providing a market for her products and services.

QUESTIONS

(a)   Describe and explain the main successes and failures of SCAP's policies in Japan.
(b)   Explain the importance of a: MacArthur, and b: The Emperor, in the period of the Occupation.

10 Women

Tokugawa Legacy

Japanese women of the Tokugawa period were the heirs to at least two traditions. One was the *samurai* family system which, superficially at least, gave women a low status and which regulated their role in society through what was known as the 'three obediences.' These 'guidelines' suggested that women should obey their fathers before marriage, obey their husbands after marriage and obey their sons after their husbands died. However, it was generally acknowledged that women's real role and power lay inside the home where they were seen as having a great deal of influence over their sons and husbands.

Another tradition was the family system practised by most Japanese. Although this varied from place to place and from generation to generation, it was, in general, much freer, and much less restricted than the *samurai* system. It was widespread among working people, tradesmen and peasants and there was much practical equality between men and women in many country areas. By the end of the Tokugawa shogunate some features of the small *samurai* elite sytstem were beginning to appear in middle class, and wealthy peasant families. However, by comparison, women in Japan were never as tightly restricted as women were in the Islamic countries of North Africa, Persia, India and South-East Asia.

Japanese girls at home in the 1890s

In the late Tokugawa period the majority of women worked in farming and fishing. Women also played a major role in the cultivation of silk. Almost all fishmongers were women, and women played an active part in the milling of grain and the transplanting of rice. Women from the countryside made up the majority of workers in Japan's early textile factories.

Meiji

The Meiji government abolished the traditional privileges of the *samurai* class, but *samurai* ideals and behaviour continued, and in the 1890s the government decided to support the old *samurai* family system as the model for society. The liberal Civil Code of 1890 was abandoned in 1892 in the face of traditional opposition, and in 1898 a revised Civil Code was introduced which established a family system based on the '*ie*' or household. The *ie* gave authority to the senior male in the family. He was made responsible for administering the family's money and affairs and for ensuring the loyalty and good behaviour of family members. The most important role of women in the *ie* was to provide a male heir to ensure the continuation of the family line.

All family properties were inherited by the eldest son, and the position of women was defined as inferior to that of men. In law a wife was regarded as unable to manage her own affairs, and could only take over the ownership of family property if there were no sons or grandsons to inherit it.

As in many European countries Japanese traditionalists saw a woman's place of work as the home, and believed that a wife should ideally be mistress of the 'inside' of the house rather than concern herself with 'outside' matters.

The concept of the *ie* or household dominated the official view of women's role in Japan from the 1890s to well into the twentieth century. The ideal woman was to be submissive, obedient, graceful and gentle. She was to be a 'good wife and wise mother.'

Apart from agriculture, the textile industry, and domestic service where women made up a major part of the workforce, there were relatively few areas of employment open to women in Meiji Japan. The upbringing of most girls did not prepare them for a professional life, and the law barred women from the civil service or becoming lawyers. However, educated women could find employment in such new modern jobs as teaching, nursing and medicine. The first Japanese woman doctor began work in 1885 and a women's medical college was opened in Tokyo in 1900. After 1868 modernisation created some openings for women as clerks, typists, telephone operators, ticket collectors and assistants in modern department stores.

Some liberal reformers campaigned against the inequality of men and women. For instance, Fukuzawa Yukichi, an important Meiji thinker and teacher, argued for equal educational opportunities for women. Christian missionaries also pioneered schools and colleges for women.

A small number of women became involved in a movement for women's political rights, but the Peace Preservation Ordinance of 1887 forbade women the right to join political parties or attend political meetings. As a result some

DOCUMENT 1   ***Things Japanese***   *Basil Hall Chamberlain (3rd edition, 1898)*

Japanese women are most womanly — kind, gentle, faithful, pretty. But the way in which they are treated by the men has hitherto been such as might cause a pang to any generous European heart. A woman's lot is summed up in what are termed 'the three obediences' — obedience, while yet unmarried, to a father; obedience, when married, to a husband and that husband's parents; obedience, when widowed, to a son. At the present moment, the greatest lady in the land may have to be a husband's drudge, to fetch and carry for him, to bow down humbly in the hall when my lord sallies forth on his walks abroad, to wait upon him at meals, to be divorced at his good pleasure....

We would not have it thought that Japanese women are actually ill-used. There is probably very little wife-beating in Japan, neither is there...any veiling of the face. Rather it is that women are all their lives treated more or less like babies....

For the sake of fairness and completeness, it should be added that the subjection of women is not carried out in the lower classes of Japanese society to the same extent as in the middle and upper. The peasant women, the wives of artisans and small traders have more liberty and a higher relative position than the great ladies of the land. In these lower classes the wife shares not only her husband's toil, but his counsels; and if she happens to have the better head of the two, she it is who will keep the purse and govern the family.

1. According to the writer in what ways did the treatment of women vary between different classes in Japan?
2. Why does the writer say that 'women are all their lives treated more or less like babies'?

women became involved in underground political movements, while other able women abandoned politics or turned to writing and literary activities.

Japan was ahead of most countries in introducing compulsory education for girls. In 1872 primary education for boys and girls began, and in the 1880s secondary education for girls started with subjects considered suitable for the training of respectful and respectable young ladies. In 1901 the Japan Women's University became the first higher education college for women and by 1912 many girls were receiving education at all levels.

A number of important social and economic changes of the time affected women. Some women in the cities, especially Tokyo, were influenced by new ideas and ways of behaviour. On the other hand, a rapid rise in the birth-rate reinforced the idea of women as mothers and home-makers. The population, which was about 30 million in the 1860s increased to nearly 50 million by 1910. At the time of the First World War the average Japanese family had five children.

Taisho

The First World War led to more rapid modernisation and gave a boost to the Japanese economy. By 1920 there were over 10 million women industrial workers, the majority employed in cotton and textile mills. Working conditions were often harsh, and most women ceased to work when they got married, or were expecting their first child. In the cities freer ideas and attitudes spread and educational opportunities increased. However, the majority of Japanese women still lived in the countryside where new styles and ways of thinking had relatively little impact.

The Suffrage Bill of 1925 gave the vote to all males over the age of 25, but women were excluded. Despite this, women's groups campaigned for the vote. In 1925 the Women's Suffrage League was formed, and in 1928 a demand for the vote signed by 32,000 women was presented to the government. After Japan's defeat in 1945 women were finally given the vote, — a few months before women received the vote in France.

Changes in women's fashion: (left) Taisho period dress showing fashionable hair-style; (right) the early Showa style. Would all women dress this way?

The Thirties and the War

During the 1930s the government made very great efforts to enforce the conservative family system. Ironically, however, the rise of nationalistic military policies helped to speed up changes in the position of women. As early as 1901 a Patriotic Women's Society had been formed to help the families and soldiers of the Sino-Japanese War, and by 1937 it had a membership of over 3 million. The society's activities were nationwide, and it ran night schools with free education for women, women's hostels, employment exchanges, day care and child health centres. A second group, the Greater Japan National Defence Women's Association, was set up in 1932, and six years later claimed 8 million members. In 1942 the two organisations were united into the Greater Japan Women's Association which had 19 million members by 1943. Under war-time regulations all women over the age of 20 were compelled to join the association. In 1941 all single women between the ages of 14 and 25 were formed into the Women's Defence League.

Social and economic conditions after 1937 changed the position of women. Despite government policy, war-time necessity made it very difficult to insist on the traditional ideal of the 'good wife and wise mother.' Labour shortages forced the recruitment of women into all areas of the Japanese economy. Many rural women were employed in munitions and aircraft factories where they did jobs previously reserved for men. By 1939 there were 1½ million women working on assembly lines in aircraft factories. However, in order to preserve traditional values, the government resisted the full mobilisation of women for the war effort until late 1943 when the desperate war situation forced them to recognise and expand the active role women were playing in the defence of the nation. In these years, transport was increasingly in the hands of women who worked as conductors, train drivers, and traffic controllers. They were employed in railway construction gangs, staffed railway stations, and some even received military training and flew aircraft to battle areas. Japanese women made a great, though largely unrecorded, contribution to the war effort.

The war was a terrible experience for most Japanese women. Queuing for food was a long, daily ritual, and with husbands drafted into the armed forces, many women had to support their families alone. Women also played a major role in air-raid defence organisations, and the air-raids in the latter part of the war added further hardship. In June 1944 all primary school children were evacuated from Tokyo to the safer country areas. Most mothers saw the air-raids and the evacuation of their children as the two most painful experiences of the war. The varied role which women played during the war probably contributed to a greater confidence in the post-war years.

Post-war Japan

Japan's defeat in 1945 heralded significant changes in the status of women. In December 1945 all women over the age of 20 were given the vote, and in April 1946 women voted for the first time. About 70% of eligible females voted, and 39 women were elected as members of the House of Representatives. The Constitution of 1947 guaranteed equal rights for men and women, and the new Civil Code abolished the *ie* and introduced the right to free choice of spouse and place of residence, and sexual equality.

These reforms marked a considerable advance in the long search for equality. However, fundamental difficulties remained and new problems emerged. As in most countries there were difficulties in changing many traditional attitudes towards women.

Politics and Government

Since the general election of 1946 the number of women members of the Diet (parliament) has declined, and in 1984 there were only 25 women out of 763 members of the two houses of the Japanese parliament. Although the voting rate of women in national elections has been higher than that of men since 1968, women's interest in politics is often low. There were virtually no women in high public office in Japan before 1945, and even today women occupy relatively few important decision-making positions. However, in this respect Japan is not greatly different from some European countries. The first female cabinet minister took office as Minister of Health and Welfare in 1960, some women have served as ambassadors, and in September 1986 the Japan Socialist Party, the major opposition party, elected a woman leader.

Marriage and Family

The post-war reforms changed the position of women within the family. The idea of a marriage between two families largely disappeared, and marriage became based on the wishes of the couple. The tradition of a wife marrying into her husband's family ended. Pre-war marriage was a joining of two families. The choice of a bride was made by the household head, and her name was only entered in the family register of her husband when she was accepted by the family as a satisfactory and dutiful wife. A new bride had to be accepted first by her father-in-law and mother-in-law. Even before 1945, however, marriage was slowly changing from one based on the family-first idea to one in which the wishes of the couple themselves received greater consideration.

Despite changes since 1945 many traditional ideas still continue. Many women and men assume that a woman's place is to be at home raising children. The use of a go-between (or introducer) in marriage is still common, particularly in rural areas. This person often arranges the first meeting of a couple in a public

---

DOCUMENT 2   **An outline plan for the reorganisation of Japan**   Kita Ikki
(1919)

Women will not have the right to participate in politics.
     The reason for the clear statement that 'Women will not have the right to participate in politics' is not that Japanese women today have not yet awakened. In medieval Japan the *samurai* esteemed and valued the person of woman on approximately the same level as they did themselves....
     There has been agitation by women for suffrage abroad while here women have continued devoted to the task of being good wives and wise mothers. Politics is a small part of human activity. The question of the place of women in Japan will be satisfactorily solved if we make an institutional reorganisation which will guarantee the protection of women's right to be 'mother of the nation and wife of the nation.' To make women accustomed to verbal warfare is to do violence to their natural aptitude; it is more terrible than using them in the line of battle. Anyone who has observed the stupid talkativeness of western women or the piercing quarrels among Chinese women will be thankful that Japanese women have continued on the right path.... The ugliness of direct and uncritical borrowing can be seen very well in the matter of woman suffrage.

1. Why did Kita feel that women should be excluded from politics?
2. Explain the significance of the phrase 'mother of the nation and wife of the nation'?
3. How successfully were women kept out of public life before 1945?

place in the company of both sets of parents. In the early 1970s over one-third of Japanese marriages were arranged in this way, and marriage in Japan has developed a dual character, with modern ideas existing alongside traditional practices.

Women's position in the home remains very strong, and often they control most of the domestic finances. Today, many Japanese husbands still hand over their pay packet to their wife unopened, although the practice is becoming less common. Wives play the major role in raising and caring for the children, a situation reinforced by the fact that in many modern Japanese households the husband spends long hours away from home, at the office or on business. Outside the home, Japanese housewives participate increasingly in varied activities. For instance, they attend meetings connected with their children's education. The average Japanese family is now much smaller than before the war. In the period 1920-1955 the average household had around 5 members; by 1980 the figure was just over 3.

Contemporary family life: (left) family meal western-style; (right) family meal traditional style on tatami. What do these pictures reveal about the modern Japanese home?

Employment

During the period of industrialisation in the nineteenth century women made up the bulk of the workforce, and from the 1850s women have been employed outside the home despite the ideal of a woman's place inside the home. The proportion of women in industry declined after the First World War, but rose dramatically after 1937.

In 1975 there were about 13½ million women in paid work in Japan, nearly 40% of the labour force. The largest number, however, are employed as family workers in small businesses or agriculture, and many do not receive a formal salary. Many women only work part-time, while it is rare for men to seek part-time employment, unless they are involved in agriculture when they seek full-time seasonal work in the towns and cities.

Young women are very visible in almost all Japanese companies

In the professions there have been some significant changes. The civil service is now open to women and about one fifth of civil servants are women. The agricultural sector of the economy is dominated by women, and in the late 1970s they made up two-thirds of agricultural workers. However, in recent years, the worlds of television and journalism have opened up new opportunities for women. Some Japanese women have now become international leaders in such fields as fashion and design. Furthermore, with increased living standards young women are enjoying leisure and foreign travel on an enormous scale.

DOCUMENT 3   ***The Women of Suye Mura***   *Robert J Smith and Ella Lury Wiswell*
(1982)

CONDITIONS IN A JAPANESE VILLAGE IN THE MID 1930s

One aspect of life in Suye Mura that may well be exceptional is the behaviour of women. Officially, as all over Japan, they occupied a subordinate position, but they did not always act as if they did. It is true that women had no role in village administrative affairs and that at home they followed the standard pattern of subservience to the husband, but in day-to-day contact with men, in their sharing of labour, in their role at social gatherings, their drinking, and their outspokenness they certainly acted with much greater freedom than any Japanese female city-dweller. One noticed this contrast immediately in observing the behaviour of the village women and that of the school teachers or the wives of school teachers who were usually city-bred women. The latter were frequently shocked by the uninhibited farmers' wives, whom they considered strange and uncouth.

1. *How can you explain the freedom of country women described here?*
2. *What were the limits to that freedom?*
3. *Do you think the village of Suye Mura was typical of Japanese villages at this time?*

The Women's Movement

The Japanese women's movement is about a hundred years old, and many of its aims have been achieved since 1945. In 1975 the government drew up a Plan of Action to improve the position of women in the next decade. This included equalisation of job opportunities, the promotion of female participation in decision-making, education and training, and improvements in maternity, health and welfare conditions for women.

Women are active in many volunteer organisations and in groups lobbying the government on the environment, education, health and other social issues. Many women are members of women's associations which give them a role outside the home. A survey in the middle 1970s estimated that nearly one quarter of all women over 20 belonged to at least one women's organisation.

The position of women in Japan has improved since the Meiji Restoration as a result of changing social and economic conditions. Women's legal rights were very limited indeed from the 1890s until 1945 but women's position slowly improved. During this time the majority of women lived and worked in the countryside.

Women have always played a major role in the Japanese economy; the development of the economy after 1868 was largely built on female labour and

---

DOCUMENT 4

Daughter-in-law speaking about her mother-in-law, c.1965 in Tsurumi Kazuko: *Social change and the individual: Japan before and after defeat in World War II* (1970)

My mother-in-law is seventy-nine years old. While she was young, she worked so hard that she could spare no time to attend any school sports, parents' meetings, women's club meetings, movies or theatres. When my eldest son entered school, I wished to go to his school to visit his class at work. But my old-fashioned mother-in-law refused to let me go, saying 'You don't have to visit your child's school every month.'

When a movie came to our district, I asked my mother-in-law to go and see the show...I encouraged her to go, saying 'It is free of admission, mother. You had better go with our neighbour.' Finally, and for the first time, she went. Since then she attends the movies whenever they come to our district hall....

She now looks forward to the movies. I also encourage her to go and attend lectures. She now goes to school sports on her own accord and has come to understand what the PTA and women's clubs are all about. She now encourages me to visit my son's class at work, to attend PTA meetings, and even to go to the public library to borrow books. I am very much impressed by the change that has come over my once old-fashioned mother-in-law.

1. *Why do you think the wife paid so much attention to the opinions of her mother-in-law?*
2. *How has the relation between the wife and her mother-in-law changed since the end of the war?*
3. *What kinds of changes do you think the mother-in-law has seen in her lifetime?*

DOCUMENT 5 · ***Letters from Sachiko: a Japanese Woman's View of Life in the Land of the Economic Miracle**   James Trager (ed) (1984)*

...Women are still looked upon as temporary employees. When times are bad the women are the first to be let go, even though they may be more competent than some men. In the short time that I spent working in an office, I saw some men who simply could not have managed if they had not had good women assistants. Some of the women told stories at lunch about supervisors who didn't seem to know what day it was, but most of us were only working until we got married so we didn't take it seriously. Not many companies hire women for professional or managerial jobs, although that is beginning to change. What generally happens is that...she often has to sign an agreement that she will retire at a certain age, or when she gets married, or when she has her first child. These agreements are not legal but thousands of women sign them and feel bound by them. So a young woman typically works for five or six years, gets married, quits work, and raises a family. She may be rehired when her children are old enough for school, and she may work for the next twenty years, but when business falls off she will find that she is expendable. Men here have job stability; women do not.

1. Why are employment conditions for women worse than conditions for men?
2. List some of the difficulties that women have to face at work.
3. How have working conditions for women changed since the Meiji Restoration?
4. How useful is this passage as a source for the historian?

Japan's war-time economy relied heavily on women. Since the early 1950s women have been a vital element in the successes of the Japanese economic miracle without achieving the job security or pay of many of their male counterparts.

Since 1945 women have largely achieved legal equality with men, but many problems remain. However, the pattern of women's lives has changed significantly. Today, women are healthier and better educated than before the war and their life expectancy at over 79 is the highest in the world. With the decline in the size of families, women have far more free time than in the past. Education for women has expanded greatly since 1945 and all national and private universities are open to women, who now make up about a third of all college and university students. Some Japanese women have reached the highest international levels in music, the arts, literature and fashion.

POINTS TO CONSIDER

1.   There were broadly two types of family systems in Tokugawa Japan; one was the *samurai* family system in which women were treated as inferior with no rights outside the home. The second was that of the majority of Japanese which was more equal and open.

2.   The Meiji government adopted the *samurai* system as the model for the nation. In theory, women were inferior to men and their realm was the family home. In practice, this ideal was difficult to enforce in a rapidly-changing Japan.

3.   Women made up the majority of the industrial workforce before World War One. They were employed in large numbers in cotton and textile mills, and increasingly in city jobs as shop girls and secretaries.

4.   In the 1930s and 1940s women played a vital role in the war industries, and began to move into jobs previously reserved for men. The war was a terrible experience for women, many of whom had to bring up families single-handed.

5.   Post-war reforms liberated women from most of the legal restrictions imposed upon them. They obtained equality with men and the right to vote, but some traditional attitudes towards women still remained.

6.   Today, women are active in all walks of Japanese life. Educational opportunities have increased dramatically, and the health and well-being of women has improved considerably since 1945. The size of the Japanese family has also changed, presenting women with new opportunities and new problems.

QUESTIONS

(a)   How realistic was the official view of women before World War Two?

(b)   What are the main problems facing women in today's Japan?

11 Growing Prosperity 1952-1970

Japan's 'bullet' train ('hikari') which runs at a top speed of 156 mph. The first section of this super-express national network (shinkansen) was opened in time for the 1964 Tokyo Olympics.

Post-Occupation Politics

Prime Minister Yoshida was still relatively popular when the peace treaty was signed in 1951. This popularity did not last long as his remote attitude turned many supporters against him. At the end of 1953 Yoshida was accused of interfering with justice when he refused to allow the arrest of the Liberal Party General Secretary for alleged bribery.

Yoshida's pro-American policy was also attacked by many Japanese. They wanted Japan to be more independent of American influence. At the same time many opposed Yoshida's attempts to reverse some Occupation reforms and return to a more centralist form of government. Yoshida believed that this was a more effective system of government but in the face of growing criticism he resigned in December 1954.

The development of the mass media helped to publicise public criticism of some government plans. The first television sets were in use in 1953 but weekly magazines were a more important influence at this time. These were very independent and were ready to attack the government or the mistakes of cabinet

Despite opposition accusations of bribery and criticisms of re-armament the conservatives remained in power. The socialist groups in the Diet gradually improved their position and united into one party in 1955. The two main conservative parties responded by joining to form the Liberal Democratic Party. This party has been in office ever since.

In the period up to 1960 there was a great deal of tension between the conservatives and the left-wing parties. The socialists feared a return to the pre-war political situation while the conservatives feared the growth of communism. In February 1957 Kishi Nobusuke became Prime Minister. He had been a member of Tojo's war-time cabinet and had been arrested as a suspected war criminal. He was a good organiser who had helped bring about the formation of the Liberal Democratic Party, but he was distrusted and disliked by many Japanese. He believed that Japan needed a strong central government, and during his time in office there were several serious confrontations with the socialists.

The socialists wanted the Occupation reforms to become an accepted part of Japanese society. The conservatives were distrusted by the opposition because they seemed to be trying to reverse these reforms. Though their changes were small compared to the Occupation reforms, these changes were in politically sensitive areas such as education and the police.

In 1956 a law was passed that ended the election of local education officials. The officials were then appointed by local government. The Ministry of Education took more control over the text books that schools were allowed to use. Later, there were widespread strikes and demonstrations when the government attempted to grade teachers on a scale of A-E. The grade that they were given was to depend on their abilities and general attitude and would determine wages and promotions. There was nationwide opposition to this plan. The teachers'

Pollution

During the 1960s general pollution of the air by car exhausts and fumes from factories became a problem throughout the urban areas of Japan. Pollution of rivers and coastal waters also increased during this period. The most famous cases of pollution occurred in the 1950s, involving the effects of cadmium and mercury poisoning.

In 1955, 32 elderly women died from cadmium poisoning in the town of Fuchu-machi, and over 200 others were affected. The side-effects of the poisoning prompted the name 'Itai Itai' disease (itai means 'painful'). The cadmium came from a mine that was discharging wastes into the river. The river water was used in rice fields and so food became contaminated. The metal gradually collected in the bones of the women and made them brittle. The painful disease developed very slowly, which is why the cause of the problem was not found for several years.

Minamata disease was caused by mercury poisoning. It was named after the city in Kyushu where more than 50 people died from the disease and many more went blind or suffered some form of brain damage. The mercury, discharged in waste water from a factory, had contaminated fish and shellfish, and most of those affected were from families of fishermen.

union argued that it was an attempt to restore political control of education. Eventually, the central system of grading was dropped in favour of compromise arrangements worked out in each local area.

The police forces were recentralised in a law passed in 1954. Later, 10,000 riot policemen were stationed in the major cities to deal with demonstrations. To some Japanese there seemed to be a danger of a return to the pre-war police system, particularly when the government introduced a bill (in 1958) to change the laws controlling the actions of police officers. The existing law did need improvement but the new law would have given the government the power to prevent demonstrations. This was seen as an attack on individual freedom and there were strikes when news spread that the government was going to try to force the bill through the Diet. The socialists refused to attend debates to discuss the bill and eventually the government was forced to drop it.

Another government move that seemed to threaten the Occupation reforms was the greater power given to the Local Government Ministry in 1956. Shortage of money also made the prefectures more dependent on central government for funds and so increased its influence in local affairs.

The government was also criticised for its build-up of the armed forces, after its establishment of the paramilitary National Police Reserve in 1950. Many argued that such action was banned by the Constitution. Others said that the existence of the Self-Defence Force was not illegal because it did not have the potential to start a war. A commission was set up to make recommendations for changing the Constitution. In fact no changes to the Constitution took place as, after the 1956 election, the Liberal Democrats did not have the two-thirds majority in the Diet that was needed for constitutional change. Though the left-wing parties gained seats in the elections of the 1950s the Liberal Democrats were able to stay in power because their political opponents were very divided.

Relations with America and the Security Treaty

Despite the peace treaty signed in San Francisco there were still American air bases and training grounds in Japan. Stories often appeared in the papers about incidents of bad behaviour by American servicemen. Such news reports had been banned during the Occupation period.

The Security Treaty was also criticised because it allowed bases in Japan to be used as staging posts for activities in other areas of Asia. The help of American troops could also be requested by the Japanese government to cope with civil disturbances. Some Japanese argued that the treaty caused difficulties in dealing with Russia and other countries in East Asia. In particular, the treaty made it difficult to restore diplomatic relations with Communist China. There was also fear that America would demand that Japan play a greater role in maintaining security in the western Pacific area. Some argued that this would not increase Japan's security, but reduce it as it would mean that Japan was clearly linked with one side in the cold war. The Constitution declared that Japan should be a peaceful nation. This suggested to many Japanese that they should not be involved in any foreign alliance.

*Prime Minister Yoshida signs the San Francisco Peace Treaty on
8 September 1951*

In 1953 Japan's Foreign Minister, Okazaki, went to the United States to try and renegotiate the inequalities of the Security Treaty. The American view was that Japan was not ready to take responsibility for its own defence. The talks ended when it seemed that any revision would include the possibility of sending Japanese troops overseas. This was totally unacceptable to most Japanese people.

Relations with America became strained further when the crew of a Japanese fishing boat were affected by radiation fall-out from a hydrogen bomb test on Bikini Atoll. One of the crew died a few months later and the incident caused widespread panic when it was realised that some of their catch of tuna had been contaminated. Understandably, Japanese public opinion was deeply disturbed.

By 1958 both Japan and the US were ready to revise the Security Treaty. In that year American ground troops left Japan. Discussions about a new treaty brought all the tensions between the conservatives and left-wing parties to a head. Although the revised treaty was more equal the socialists wanted it scrapped altogether, arguing that there was a risk of Japan becoming involved in an American war in Asia. There were months of negotiations before the terms of the new security pact were announced. It was to remain in force for ten years. The new pact was signed in Washington but still had to be passed through the Diet.

The socialists tried to prevent the pact being accepted by holding it up in committee discussions for three months. The Liberal Democrats responded by forcing a sudden vote late on the evening of 19 May 1960. Despite socialist opposition it was decided to extend the session by fifty days to discuss the bill. The timing of this move meant that the bill would automatically become law if it was passed in the Lower House. This avoided having to pass it through the Upper House of the Diet. The socialist members started sit-down strikes to block the entrance and corridors of the Diet buildings and so prevent the session taking place. They were forcibly removed by police guards. The bill was passed in a few minutes, just after midnight on 20 May.

People were shocked throughout Japan. Even those in favour of the new treaty were opposed to the methods that the government had used to pass the bill. There was a national railway strike and mass demonstrations by students and all types of ordinary people. Sometimes, there were violent clashes with the police and in one incident a girl was crushed to death outside the Diet building. At times, there were 100,000 people marching in the streets of Tokyo. An emergency cabinet meeting on 16 June decided to cancel the planned visit of American President Eisenhower. The conservatives had been shown that they could not ignore public opinion which regarded Kishi's behaviour as undemocratic in spirit.

Prime Minister Kishi resigned, taking public responsibility for the disturbances. Despite this, the Liberal Democrats were returned to power with a substantial majority in the elections in the autumn of 1960.

Prime Minister Ikeda (1960-64) and the National Income Doubling Plan

Ikeda followed Kishi as prime minister of Japan in autumn 1960. During his four years in office there were no major political struggles with the socialists. Ikeda's approach was quite different from that of Kishi. He cooperated with the opposition parties. This was easier now that new leaders were emerging who had not been important figures in pre-war politics. After the 1960 treaty crisis Ikeda was sensitive to popular opinion and recognised that this style of government had been clearly demanded by the press. Ikeda had been Minister of Finance and Minister of International Trade and Industry. He had a thorough understanding of the working of the economy and he appealed to the Japanese people to support him in an effort to double the national income within ten years. Most Japanese

RELATIVE POSITIONS OF GROSS NATIONAL PRODUCTS OF SELECTED COUNTRIES (1951-1982)

	Japan		U.S.A.		Germany, F.R.		France		U.K.	
	Amount (US$ billion)	Index (U.S.A =100)	Amount (US$ billion)	Index (U.S.A =100)	Amount (US$ billion)	Index (U.S.A =100)	Amount (US$ billion)	Index (U.S.A =100)	Amount (US$ billion)	Index (U.S.A =100)
1951	14.2	4.3	328.4	100.0	28.5	8.7	35.1	10.7	41.4	12.6
1955	22.7	5.7	398.0	100.0	43.0	10.8	49.2	12.4	53.9	13.5
1960	39.1	7.8	503.8	100.0	70.7	14.0	60.0	11.9	71.9	14.3
1965	88.8	12.9	688.1	100.0	115.1	16.7	99.2	14.4	100.2	14.6
1970	203.1	20.5	992.7	100.0	184.6	18.6	145.5	14.7	124.0	12.5
1975	498.2	32.2	1,549.2	100.0	418.2	27.0	339.7	21.9	234.5	15.1
1978	963.3	44.5	2,163.8	100.0	642.2	29.7	476.6	22.0	318.6	14.7
1979	998.9	41.3	2,417.8	100.0	761.3	31.5	576.6	23.8	412.2	17.0
1980	1,040.1	39.5	2,633.1	100.0	816.5	31.0	657.1	25.0	525.5	20.0
1981	1,139.3	38.8	2,937.7	100.0	682.8	23.2	572.6	19.5	504.3	17.2
1982	1,060.0	34.6	3,059.3	100.0	659.4	21.6	—	—	473.8	15.5

Note: Current U.S. dollar figures are calculated according to the annual average exchange rates of the IMF, *International Financial Statistics* (refer to table 6-7). U.S.A = 100 for all years.

The opening ceremony of the Tokyo Olympics (1964). What was so significant about the games being held in Japan?

were keen to support this plan, when it was announced in September 1960. They used their energies to improve their own, and their nation's wealth. The main concerns became economic progress and national pride rather than re-armament and a centralised government.

The socialists were divided over the Security Treaty and broke into two parties before the elections of 1960. In later elections they received a smaller share of the vote and this meant they could not hope to take power. Most Japanese were happy to support the Liberal Democrats as long as they responded to public opinion. The government gained further encouragement when Japan's progress was noted in the West and the growing prosperity at home became obvious. Japan's peaceful policies and economic success were symbolised by the holding of the Olympic Games in Tokyo in 1964.

Ikeda's policies were effective because they followed a trend that was already developing. By the mid-1950s Japan had reached its pre-war economic levels. Techniques for making cars, watches, cameras and ships that had been developed during the war and Occupation, were employed to build up Japan's economy. By 1965 Japan was producing half of the new shipping tonnage of the world. In the same year, Japan exported more than she imported for the first time since the war. This export surplus increased sharply in the next few years.

A number of factors help to explain Japan's economic success in the 1950s. Japan concentrated on importing technology from more advanced nations, rather than spending vast sums on research. Its labour force was highly educated and Japan spent a much smaller proportion of the national income on defence than most western countries. The government supported growing industries by a policy of protection. Many foreign imports were restricted by tariffs and rigorous checks. The Ministry of Finance and the Ministry of International Trade and Industry

(MITI) set priorities and directed banks to lend money to develop particular industries.

By the end of the 1960s evidence of prosperity was obvious everywhere. Cars, colour televisions and air conditioning were common, while people started to take foreign holidays. Modern roads covered the country and the towns had grown dramatically in size as people moved to urban areas to find work in factories and offices. International recognition of Japan's international achievements and new importance was shown when the World Exposition was held at Osaka in 1970.

Relations with Russia

It was not until 1955 that international tension eased enough for Japan and Russia to begin negotiations on a form of peace treaty. The Japanese attitude towards Russia up to that time was one of fear and dislike. Russian forces had occupied the southern half of Sakhalin, the Kuriles and four other islands close to the north coast of Japan in 1945. The Soviet Union had also mistreated large numbers of Japanese prisoners of war.

The Russians were in a strong position in the negotiations that took place in 1956. They could block Japan's entry to the United Nations and they controlled access to some of Japan's old fishing grounds. After several months, negotiations ended because there was no agreement over the territorial issue. Russia had offered to return two small islands to Japanese control, but the Japanese argued that two more islands were also historically Japanese territories. Despite these problems a settlement was reached over trade and normal diplomatic relations were resumed in October 1956. However there was no formal peace treaty. The

Post-war Prime Ministers

Prince Higashikuni	1945-
Baron Shidehara Kijuro	1945-1946
Yoshida Shigeru	1946-1947
Katayama Tetsu	1947-1948
Ashida Hitoshi	1948-
Yoshida Shigeru	1948-1954
Hatoyama Ichiro	1954-1956
Ishibashi Tanzan	1956-1957
Kishi Nobusuke	1957-1960
Ikeda Hayato	1960-1964
Sato Eisaku	1964-1972
Tanaka Kakuei	1972-1974
Miki Takeo	1974-1976
Fukuda Takeo	1976-1978
Ohira Masayoshi	1978-1980
Suzuki Zenko	1980-1982
Nakasone Yasuhiro	1982-1987
Takeshita Noboru	1987-

following month, Japan became a member of the United Nations.

Relations with Russia remained strained for the next few years. There were disputes over fishing grounds around the Kuriles, and incidents when Russian warships seized Japanese fishing vessels.

In the 1960s relations improved a little as Russia wanted loans and technological assistance in developing its Far-Eastern territories. The Japanese were offered oil and other raw materials in return for this assistance. This was at a time when there was growing hostility between Russia and China.

Relations with China

As a result of pressure from Japanese companies the government had relaxed rules about trading with Communist China in the 1950s and this made some unofficial dealings possible. Trade slowly increased but was broken off when Japan made it clear that trade agreements did not mean that Japan could formally recognise the People's Republic of China. Japan, like America, only recognised the Nationalist Chinese government in Taiwan. Japan did not want to risk its well-developed trade with Taiwan nor did it want to offend the United States by changing this policy.

The Ikeda government resumed trade relations with communist China. Ikeda's policy was to separate trade from politics and by 1965 Japan was China's main trading partner. Russian advisers had left China in 1960 and Japan was looked on as a new source of technology and economic assistance.

Relations became more difficult during the time that Prime Minister Sato was in office (1964-72). In 1964 China began testing atomic weapons and in 1966 the country was thrown into turmoil by the Cultural Revolution. When the war in Vietnam developed to involve American troops, for a time, some people feared that Japan could become involved in a war with China which was supporting North Vietnam. As a result of these strains in relations between Tokyo and Beijing (Peking), trade and other connections almost ceased. Despite these problems many Japanese felt they should recognise the People's Republic of China just as Britain and Canada had done. There was a feeling that Japan was neglecting her own interests by following the American lead too closely.

Japan and the Pacific Region

During the 1960s Japan made a conscious attempt to build better relations with its neighbours in Asia. The government was aware that Japan's international position could be improved by trade links with the other nations of the Pacific region. In the post-war period attempts to revive trade with Korea, Australia and other nations were hindered by feelings of suspicion remaining from the war.

Japan paid reparations to countries that it had occupied in Asia. In 1961 Prime Minister Ikeda visited Pakistan, India, Burma and Thailand and agreement was reached on the level of reparations to these countries. Most of these payments were in the form of goods and services and they helped to provide valuable orders for Japanese companies. They also formed the basis of future trade. The reparations were followed by aid and loans. Japanese companies invested heavily in developing factories and supplies of raw material and by the mid 1960s Japan was the main economic power of the Pacific region.

Relations with Japan's former colony South Korea were not normalised until 1965. This was after disagreements over fishing rights and the level of reparations had been settled. Once trade between the two countries resumed, Korea benefited from further economic growth.

Okinawa and Vietnam

American military bases in Okinawa completely dominated the islands and their society in the 1950s. By the 1970s most Japanese felt that Okinawa should return to their administration. In 1961 Ikeda visited America and discussed the problem with President Kennedy. As a result, agreements were reached for cooperation between the two governments to safeguard the welfare of the people of Okinawa, and they were allowed to fly the Japanese flag for the first time since the war. Sato was the first post-war Prime Minister to visit the islands. In 1969 he negotiated an agreement whereby Okinawa would return to Japan in 1972.

Japan's economy benefited from the war in Vietnam but government support for American policies in Asia was often unpopular. Television and newspapers showed the horrors of the Vietnam war and Japanese sometimes sympathised with the plight of fellow Asians caught up in the fighting. At the same time there was a fear that the conflict could spread to involve China and might lead to a nuclear war.

EXPO '70, Osaka. The exposition lasted six months and attracted exhibitors from all over the world

POINTS TO CONSIDER

1.   The period from 1952-1960 was one where issues left over from the war and Occupation were still important.
2.   Up to 1960 there was deep mistrust between the left-wing parties and the conservatives.
3.   Before 1960 party leaders included some who had been prominent in politics before the war.
4.   Until 1960 there seemed a strong possibility that the Occupation reforms would be reversed.
5.   Negotiation of a more equal Security Treaty with the United States was a major aim of the post-Occupation governments.
6.   After 1960 government policies were dominated by concern with economic development.

QUESTIONS:

(a)   Describe the domestic policies of the Japanese government from 1952-70. How were they viewed by the Japanese people?
(b)   Compare Japan's relations with Russia and China in this period.

12 Post-war Industry

Introduction

By the end of the Second World War much of Japan's industry was in ruins. Factories and communications had been damaged or destroyed by American bombing and naval bombardment. There was a shortage of raw materials and much skilled labour had been conscripted into the armed forces. With the ending of war, a great deal of industrial production had come to a halt. The immediate post-war years were characterised by confusion, apathy, food shortages and inflation.

At first, the Occupation authorities (SCAP — Supreme Commander for the Allied Powers) decided to dismantle much of Japan's war industry and break up the pre-war industrial combines (*zaibatsu*). SCAP believed that the *zaibatsu* had cooperated actively with the military to build up Japan's war machine, and were therefore obstacles to democracy and free competition. In December 1946 the Pauley mission recommended that many of Japan's industrial plants should be dismantled and given as reparations to the Asian countries that had been occupied by the Japanese. However, these proposals were not carried out. In fact, by 1948, America was encouraging Japan's efforts at industrial recovery.

By the late 1960s the shipbuilding industry had entered the age of mammoth tankers with Japanese yards leading the way in building the world's first 300,000-ton vessels

In the late 1960s Japan had recovered from the disasters of the war and was already the third greatest industrial power in the world, after the United States and the Soviet Union. Her standard of living was equal to the leading countries of Western Europe, and she was among the world's leading producers of steel, televisions, radios, ships, and cars. Most of these industries had been of little importance before the war.

The history of Japanese industry since 1945 can be divided roughly into three main phases. The first phase, lasting from 1945 to about 1955, was a time of confusion followed by reconstruction. The second phase, from 1955 to the early 1970s, saw the dramatic growth and expansion of industry as Japan became an economic giant. In the final phase, from the early 1970s to the present, Japan attempted to adjust her industry to the two oil crises, new competitors and a decline in the importance of such heavy industries as iron, steel and shipbuilding.

Confusion and Reconstruction: 1945-1955

The years 1945 to 1948 were a period of confusion in Japan, as SCAP attempted to break up the biggest *zaibatsu* and make Japan's economic and political system more competitive and democratic. It was not until 1948 and 1949 that major steps were also taken to begin the reconstruction of industry. In the early years recovery was very slow, and in 1948 industrial productivity was only about 40% of what it had been in 1937.

Measures were taken to remove the business leaders who had been closely linked with the war. Steps were also taken to break up the biggest *zaibatsu*. The aim of this programme was to destroy the wealth and power of *zaibatsu* families, and to break each group into several independent enterprises. Consequently, family leadership of these groups was ended. Many top managers resigned and many of the ties holding the different branches of the groups together were broken. However, changing local and international circumstances finally halted the programme. In Japan, it was feared that post-war economic hardships were

---

DOCUMENT 1

Testimony of an electrician *working at Matsushita's TV assembly plant in Puerto Rico (1970s)*

This is a remarkable company. When they first came, we were struck by their production control system and the importance of achieving results. They sent 100 workers to Japan to see how plants worked there. They have an open door to management and really encourage suggestions. Every morning we have meetings and we all recite the seven values of Matsushita. It seemed silly at first. This was a sloppy, losing operation before they acquired it. When they came in, they said they wanted to turn a profit within three years, and — by God — we made it.

1. *Why was Matsushita so successful in Puerto Rico?*
2. *What is the importance of the suggestion system in Japanese companies?*

pushing the trade unions and workers into more and more radical views, and creating the danger of a revolution. Abroad, the bad relations between the United States and the USSR and the approaching victory of the communists in the Chinese Civil War made it vital that Japan should be rebuilt as an American ally in Asia. These changes made the dissolution of the *zaibatsu* seem economically harmful. It was obvious that Japan would need large firms to help revive her economy and by 1949 it was decided that the dissolution plans should not be extended. In the late 1950s some of the pre-war groups re-emerged in very much looser form. However, they were now challenged by new post-war firms who were powerful competitors.

The first industries to become active after the war were such light industries as textiles, and the heavy industries iron, steel and electric power generation. However, many industries had problems of out-of-date, or damaged, equipment, and had lost the markets formerly provided by the military and Japan's colonies. The problem of re-equipping factories was partly solved by American financial and technical aid. Japan also had a large supply of willing and qualified workers who were able to adapt themselves to new industries and assembly-line techniques. In the late 1940s and early 1950s a number of industries which had their origins in the pre-war economy began to prosper. Among these were firms making

---

DOCUMENT 2   *Hitachi Union Song*

The storm still blows, the mountain pass is long
But we will never give up.
Though still the sun gives no glimpse of light
Dawn approaches for the working man.
Our Hitachi! Hitachi where the muscles tense!
Never slacken. Shoulder to shoulder we move ahead.
Soon you shall see! Soon you shall see!
The path is dark, precipitous. Cold penetrates the bone
But no one walks alone.
Though still the sun gives no glimpse of light
Somewhere, faintly, the first cock crows.
Our Hitachi! Hitachi where the muscles tense!
In amity and unison, with laughter and song we move ahead.
Soon you shall see! Soon you shall see!
Now to be born anew; the history of Japan.
Wave the union flag on high.
The sun thrusts up over the horizon
The century of the working man arrives!
Our Hitachi! Hitachi where the muscles tense!
Grit teeth, tighten belts, just one more short haul
Soon you shall see! Soon you shall see!

1. *What is the purpose of such a song?*
2. *In what ways do Japanese unions differ from those in the West?*

cameras and electrical goods. Now these industries adapted themselves to new markets, and the photographic industry in particular developed rapidly. In these years, firms such as Nikon of Tokyo and Minolta of Osaka began to assume a world position which they have never lost.

In the late 1940s there was a considerable debate among industrialists and politicians over the best industrial policy for Japan. Although Japan had a large, skilled labour force and an ample supply of industrial managers and administrators, she lacked both raw materials for heavy industry, and capital. It seemed that the best policy might be to continue with the pre-war pattern and concentrate on light industries and agriculture. The pre-war development of heavy industry had been very costly and had only been sustained through military orders and the protected markets of the empire. These ideas were strongly opposed by the Ministry of International Trade and Industry (MITI) which was set up in 1949. MITI argued that as much capital as possible should be put into the heavy and chemical industries. This would require considerable investment but the profits would be far bigger than from any policy built on light industry and agriculture. By the early 1950s the government had accepted the MITI argument. In 1949 the American, Joseph Dodge, had come to Japan to advise SCAP and introduce reforms that cut public spending and brought inflation under control. Industry was already beginning to recover when the Korean war began.

The outbreak of the Korean war in 1950 helped to ensure that the debate over industrial policy would conclude that the first priority was heavy industry. The war was a major turning point in Japan's industrial recovery, as demand for lorries, tools and spare parts for military equipment and aircraft stimulated the rebirth of Japanese heavy industry. During the early 1950s billions of dollars flooded in as Japan became the workshop for the United Nations forces in Korea. The Korean war helped to shift the emphasis of government policy to economic growth, and laid the foundation and provided the money for future industrial development.

Industrial Giant: 1955-1973

Japan's remarkable industrial expansion after the mid 1950s was motivated largely by the desire to 'catch up' with the advanced western nations, especially the United States. Her expansion was the result of a wide variety of factors. Japan had a pre-war industrial base which provided the framework for expansion, while the war destroyed much out-of-date plant and equipment. The expansion of the world economy in the 1950s gave new opportunities for industrial growth, and the break-up of the *zaibatsu* encouraged intense competition within Japanese industry. Japan did not have to waste scarce resources on supporting large military forces, and she was able to buy technical know-how from the West relatively easily and cheaply, thereby avoiding expensive research and development costs. In 1938 Japan spent 16% of her wealth on military needs, thirty years later she spent a mere 0.8%. At first, Japan made use of imported technology. Later, she developed her own products. Japan already possessed a skilled and educated workforce which had long experience of working in industry. The countryside

A car assembly line of the 1970s. What differences, if any, would you expect to see on an assembly line of the 1980s?

provided a valuable supply of new workers. A new generation of business leaders emerged who saw growth as more important than fast profits, and who emphasised quality control and their share of the market. Industry was able to obtain large amounts of money for investment from the large personal savings of ordinary Japanese.

The government played a key role in helping industrial growth with the philosophy 'Export or die.' Although economic planning was not centrally directed as in Eastern Europe, nevertheless, the government took strong action to steer the economy in directions it favoured. It achieved this by a complex mixture of planning, rewards, persuasion and control. The Economic Planning Agency was set up to oversee the general direction of industrial policy, and it issued national economic plans which were a strong indication to industry of the government's wishes. The government, largely represented by MITI and the Ministry of Finance, had very close relations with private business and the banks, and industrialists were usually willing to follow government suggestions. The government also protected certain industries from foreign competition by imposing import controls, and encouraged the growth of key industries by giving them special tax relief and financial assistance. In general, this kind of help was given to new industries which used imported technology and were likely to become successful exporters.

The first priority was the development of heavy industry and, until the late 1960s, special encouragement was given to industries such as iron and steel, shipbuilding, commercial vehicles, and TV and radio. Once these industries were established, the government shifted its attention to industries that had not been very important before the war — such as private cars, computer equipment and petrochemicals. Within this policy MITI also gave help to important small companies. The government spent relatively little on defence, health, welfare, or social security, and gave very little assistance to industries that were inefficient or had little export potential.

A good example of the success of this strategy is the car industry. Before the war Japan had built very few cars, and in 1960 she only produced 500,000 annually, although she was a leading producer of motor cycles. Protected by a tariff wall, within five years Japan's car production leapt to 2 million, and by the end of the 1960s she was the world's second biggest car producer after the United States.

As industry began to grow rapidly in the late 1950s and early 1960s, business confidence grew. This encouraged more investment and more enterprises, a large number of which were successful. By the mid-1960s as much as 40% of Japan's national income was being invested in new ideas, plant and machinery, while the demand for goods was supported by an expanding home market and growing markets abroad.

GROWTH TRENDS OF REAL PER CAPITAL GNP (1880-1980)
(USA 1980=100)

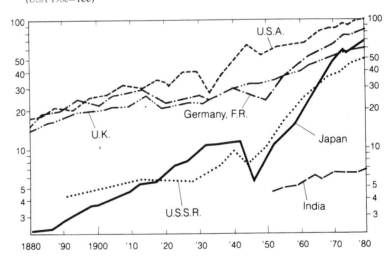

Industrial Location and Pollution

Since the 1880s the bulk of Japan's industries have been concentrated along the Pacific coast, from the Tokyo area southwards to Kyushu. The large conurbations of Tokyo-Yokohama, Osaka-Kobe, and Nagoya contain the largest proportion of industry. Since 1945 this pattern has not changed significantly, but there have been changes within this industrial area. In general, heavy industries such as iron and steel, and petrochemicals have spread along the coast, often on reclaimed land, while assembly-line industries such as cars and television have been located on inland sites, on the fringes of the major conurbations. Today, only the western part of the Japan Sea coast, southern Shikoku, much of the southern island of Kyushu and northern and eastern Hokkaido are relatively free of industrial activity.

Since 1965, Japanese industry has faced a growing problem of traffic congestion slowing down the distribution of goods and materials. To combat this many firms began to move their products by night. By the early 1960s Japan's rapid economic growth was producing serious atmospheric pollution from cars, oil refineries and petrochemical industries, and iron and steel works. The problem was made worse by the fact that many industrial zones were located very near to residential districts. In some areas large numbers of people suffered from pollution-related diseases. This caused growing public concern about the human and environmental costs of rapid industrial growth.

In the late 1960s and early 1970s industry began to expand into more and more rural areas. The move was prompted by the availability of labour in the countryside, and the growth of the motorway system after 1964. This meant that

---

DOCUMENT 3   *Building a New Japan: a plan for remodelling the Japanese archipelago*   Tanaka Kakuei (1972)

It is possible to transform Japan into a richer, less polluted, and more livable land than it is now. To do this, however, it is necessary to divert the historical trend concentrating industry, population, and culture in the major urban areas and to refocus the development emphasis on outlying regions.

In so doing, long-term and comprehensive planning...is most important. At the same time, it would also be effective to locate new industries and relocate existing industries to local areas in line with those areas' developmental potential. Industry is both the detonator and guiding force for regional development.

What I mean here by industrial relocation is to halt the flow of industry into the Pacific coastal region and to actively divert industry from the overcrowded urban areas to rural sites. In other words, this means taking from Tokyo, Osaka, and other urban concentrations their traditional industrial function and dispersing these industries....

Thus the redistribution of industry is an integral and pivotal part of the comprehensive national development plan including building a nation-wide network of super-express railways, providing expressways and other highway transport facilities, constructing connecting bridges between Shikoku and Honshu, forming a nation-wide information and communications network, protecting the environment, redeveloping our urban areas, creating regional urban centres, and restoring Japanese agriculture.

1. Why was a 'comprehensive national development plan' considered necessary in the early 1970s?
2. Where are the major concentrations of industry in Japan?
3. Why were some points of the plan achieved and others ignored?
4. What happened to the author in the years immediately after this document was published?

Port Island, Kobe, completed in 1981; the second island, Rokko Island, is under construction (top right). Why is this second island so called?

it was no longer necessary to site new industry so close to major centres of population. In 1972, Prime Minister Tanaka announced his plan for remodelling Japan by spreading industry more widely and reducing pollution. However, inflation and the oil shock of 1973 caused much of the plan to be abandoned. Laws controlling very bad cases of pollution were passed.

Trade Unions and Management

Unions were severely controlled by pre-war governments, and banned altogether in 1940. At first, SCAP believed that a strong trade union movement was necessary if Japan was to be democratic, and laws permitting unions and protecting workers' rights were passed in 1946 and 1947. Immediately after the war the movement expanded rapidly, but SCAP's anti-union measures of 1948-9 weakened it.

Most Japanese unions are company unions, and workers in a particular company or plant are organised in one union. The company union includes both shop-floor workers and administrative and management staff, and is responsible for all matters concerning wages and conditions of its members. Many company unions are affiliated to one of the national union federations of which the biggest is Sohyo (Japan Trade Unions General Council) which is closely linked with the Japan Socialist Party. However, the national federations do not play a significant role in the day-to-day affairs of workers, although they are responsible for organising the so-called 'Spring Offensive' every year at which new wage levels are set.

Only about 30% of Japanese workers are unionised, and union activity is confined to workers in large firms and the public sector. Numbers fell in the 1950s. Membership increased again in the 1960s, and by 1983 numbered 12½ million.

DOCUMENT 4   **'Clash of the titans'** *Economist 23-29 August 1986*

In the 1960s, American companies held all the technological high cards and dominated the world's markets for manufactured goods. The United States supplied over three-quarters of the television sets, half the motor cars and a quarter of the steel used around the world. Yet, a mere two decades later, Japan had taken America's place as the dominant supplier of such products.

Angry and confused, businessmen in the United States have had to stand by and watch as 'smokestack' industry all around them has been snuffed out. Then came the unthinkable: if the Japanese could thrash them in mainstream manufacturing, would they give them a mauling in high technology too?

By the beginning of the 1980s, it began to look as if they would. It became clear that the Ministry of International Trade and Industry (MITI) in Tokyo had 'targeted' not just semiconductors and computers but all of America's high-technology industries — from aerospace to synthetic materials — for a blitzkrieg attack.

Six years on, Japan has scored some notable hits. A group of American economists and engineers met for three days at Stanford University, California, last year to assess the damage. They concluded that Japanese manufacturers were already ahead in consumer electronics, advanced materials and robotics, and were emerging as America's fiercest competitors in such lucrative areas as computers, telecommunications, home and office automation, biotechnology and medical instruments. 'In other areas in which Americans still hold the lead, such as semiconductors and optoelectronics, American companies are hearing the footsteps of the Japanese,' commented the Stanford economist Mr Daniel Okimoto.

1. *What is meant by 'smokestack' industry?*
2. *Why do American high-technology companies fear Japanese competition?*
3. *Imagine you are a Japanese journalist. Write a short article on the same subject for a magazine in Tokyo.*

Japanese workers have made a significant contribution to industrial growth since 1945. In general, they have displayed a high degree of discipline and loyalty, and Japan was relatively free of major disputes through the 1950s and 1960s. The fact that most unions are company unions helped to strengthen workers' identification with the company, and loyalty to it.

The attitudes of management also played a major role in ensuring that labour disputes did not significantly hold back economic progress. One of the important features of Japanese industry is the use of an intensive system of discussion about company policies and work processes before any important decisions are made. A great deal of consultation takes place before new policies are introduced, but once a policy is decided it can be carried out as a decision of the whole company, and not simply of the management. Workers are encouraged to make suggestions about how their company can be made more efficient, and prizes and bonuses are regularly given to the best suggestions. Managers usually wear the same uniform as shop-floor workers, and are expected to spend some time working on

Building workers exercising at the start of the working day. What other information about contemporary life in Japan does this picture provide?

the shop floor. Workers and managers share the same canteen and leisure facilities. In these ways, workers and management can feel part of the same team, and are encouraged to work together for the benefit of the company and themselves.

Dual Industrial Structure

The backbone of the Japanese economy is made up of small businesses working for the domestic market. Most of Japan's industry is small and little concerned with exporting. Nearly three-quarters of all Japanese workers are employed in small or medium-scale businesses, employing less than 300 workers, and there is a considerable gap between the wages and conditions of workers in the large companies and the rest. In 1984, the average wage in small firms was only about two-thirds of that of large companies. In addition, a worker in a large company receives a wider range of benefits and bonuses. The large firms are able to recruit the most able graduates from the best universities, while the smaller companies have to make do with less successful graduates. Company loyalty is more difficult to achieve in these companies, and use is often made of 'temporary' workers who can be dropped when business is slack.

DOCUMENT 5   ***The Sun at Noon: An Anatomy of Modern Japan***
Dick Wilson (1986)

...Productivity throughout Japan — especially in agriculture and services — is lower than in America or Europe. Morita of Sony concedes that in the sectors where American productivity is weak, it is not inherent labour attitudes but poor management that is to blame; the American sense of duty, once harnessed, is stronger than Japan's. Japan has had to sacrifice and struggle for the productivity gains she has made in industry, and will have an uphill task to retain them in the future.

What group feeling and emotional motivation on the Japanese factory floor can produce is not just a good industrial atmosphere but more effective procedures. Take the question of flexibility and mobility of labour. As a late developer, Japan was able to avoid some of the dated ideas developed in Britain, such as craft apprenticeship, which compartmentalises skills — and job specification, which unnecessarily complicates production. Workers move around a Japanese plant, getting a variety of experience which makes them versatile. Specialists and technicians may bounce out of the office area to circulate on the factory floor, encouraging the development of new products and ideas. All these things can be done without suspicion or resentment of the kind that would occur in some western factories.

1. What are some of the reasons for Japan's industrial success suggested in the passage?
2. What benefits did Japan gain from starting to industrialise after Britain?
3. Why is Japanese productivity lower than the West in agriculture and services (= industries that provide services rather than manufactured goods, e.g. hotels and catering)?

There is a close relationship between many of the large industrial firms and the smaller companies, and the large companies contract work out to the small businesses. In fact, the major assembly-line industries rely heavily on a large number of small-parts manufacturers. Major car plants, for example, purchase over 70% of their components from outside firms. It is the small industries that suffer first when a large firm or the economy is in difficulties. Japan, in fact, has been described as a 'nation of small shopkeepers, family businesses and minuscule sub-contractors.' Although companies such as Toyota, Nissan, Sony, Hitachi, and Toshiba are well known to consumers in the West, it is in the close relationship between the small businesses and the industrial giants that Japanese economic strength lies. The well-known benefits of life-time employment are a feature of large but not small firms.

Period of Adjustment, 1973-

Japan's industrial prosperity of the 1960s was built partly on the availability of cheap raw materials and energy, and 60% of her energy needs were supplied by crude oil. The price of imported oil fell after 1955 and the output from the Middle East's oilfields increased dramatically. The development of extremely large 'supertankers' helped to keep the cost of transporting oil low. However, the price of oil began to rise in the late 1960s as a result of developments in the Middle East, and in 1973 the price of oil rocketed, causing a major crisis for Japanese industry. These events, known in Japan as the 'Oil shock,' signalled the end of the era of very high economic growth. In 1974 the Japanese economy was static for the first time since the late 1950s, and in the following year there was only a small increase in GNP.

The 'Oil shock' forced government and industry to consider their industrial strategies. The days of unlimited growth based on cheap oil were over and ways were needed to overcome Japan's dependence on imported raw materials. The need to meet this challenge was encouraged by a number of other factors. The period of rapid industrial growth had caused human and environmental damage and there was new opposition to the idea of 'growth at any price.' Even before the 'Oil shock', opinion suggested that the government should devote more energy and funds to provide social and welfare services, particularly in view of Japan's ageing population. There were also problems of American pressure to increase military expenditure, and pressure from Europe and the United States over Japan's trade surplus. All these problems which had begun to appear in the late 1960s needed answers.

The crisis of 1973-4 and the response to it marked the beginning of a new period in Japan's industrial and economic history. Despite suggestions that Japan was facing an economic disaster after the quadrupling of Middle East oil prices, Japanese industry recovered remarkably quickly. Within two years the economy began to grow again at a satisfactory rate and, although the very high annual production increases of the 1960s have not returned, Japan responded more successfully to the oil crisis of the 1970s than many of its competitors.

A precision assembly robot inserting integrated circuits (IC's) on printed wiring boards. In 1982 Japan exported 24,000 industrial robots of which 20% were assembly robots

The oil shocks prompted a search for new sources of oil and increased investment in alternative energy sources such as hydro-electricity, solar and wave power, and nuclear energy. At present, Japan sees its nuclear energy programme as vital until new more reliable sources of energy can be developed and exploited. In 1984 Japan had 27 nuclear power stations in operation, 13 under construction and 4 planned.

By the late 1970s there was a significant move away from the traditional 'smoke-stack' or heavy industries which rely so much on imported raw materials and energy. Such industries, for example, the iron and steel and shipbuilding industries are now in relative decline. The growth of competition from newly industrialising countries (NICs) such as Taiwan, South Korea and Brazil also stimulated this change. The 1980s have seen the growth of technologically sophisticated industries which require considerable amounts of research and capital, but have low material and energy costs, such as computers, micro-electronics, fibre optics, and bio-technology. Today, Japanese industry is once again adjusting itself to new challenges, developing new skills and opening new markets. However, there is no easy solution to the problems of harmonising industrial growth and environmental needs, and — increasing exports while keeping on friendly terms with foreign countries.

Fukushima Daiichi nuclear power station, consisting of six units with a total output of 4,696 megawatts, is the largest nuclear power station in the world. By 1995 Japan intends to increase nuclear energy to 14% of the total primary energy supply (1984: 8.2%)

POINTS TO CONSIDER

1.   Industry was in ruins in 1945 and the early post-war years saw only a slow rebuilding. SCAP began to dismantle the *zaibatsu* and relatively little attention was given to rebuilding Japanese industry.

2.   Changing local and international circumstances stimulated the reconstruction of industry after 1948. The Korean War had a profound affect on the rebirth of heavy industry.

3.   In the 1950s Japan's industrial strategy was built on capital-intensive heavy industry, and in the early 1960s a move towards developing consumer industries began.

4.   The government played a key role in directing industry, through MITI and the Ministry of Finance. Trade unions and management generally cooperated in the efficient running of large companies.

5.   Although large Japanese firms are well known internationally, the bulk of Japanese industry is small-scale and not directly involved in exporting. Small businesses make up the backbone of the economy, using non-union labour and temporary workers.

6.   The oil shocks of the 1970s caused a fundamental readjustment in industry, with new industries such as electronics and telecommunications taking over from the declining heavy industries such as iron, steel and shipbuilding.

QUESTIONS

(a)   How was Japanese industry able to recover from the destruction of the war and become an industrial giant?

(b)   What was the effect of the 1973 oil shock on industry?

13 Japan Today

Prosperity and its Problems

By the beginning of the 1970s many Japanese were enjoying prosperity for the first time. However, some also started to question the need for unrestrained, economic growth. These Japanese were concerned about the effects that the rapid expansion of industry was having on the environment and the quality of life. One of these effects was a chronic housing shortage in the big cities. Government plans to provide new homes did little to solve this. After great numbers of people had moved to the cities in the 1960s Japan contained some of the most densely-populated areas in the world. Pressure on the cities was enormous with one in every nine people living in the capital, and a quarter of the whole population having their homes in the industrial belt that stretches from Tokyo to Osaka.

In 1970 magazines and newspapers began to print articles about the effects of pollution. There had been dramatic cases of cadmium and mercury poisoning during the 1950s and 1960s but now there was a popular reaction against the more general effects of pollution. The air, rivers and seas were often affected and the 'smog' in Tokyo became a serious problem. Citizen protest groups began

Central Tokyo's expressway system — built in the 1960s but overcrowded in the 1980s and frequently reducing traffic to Tokyo's average vehicle speed of 8mph

to take legal action against companies that were damaging people's health through pollution. They often won sympathetic judgements in the courts.

Some Japanese felt that the government was too closely associated with business interests to tackle the pollution problem effectively. In the early 1970s radical governors in Tokyo, Osaka and Kyoto were often more active than the government in dealing with environmental problems. From 1971 the government enforced the Waste Management and Public Cleansing Law, but it was many years before pollution was halted and its effect on the environment began to be reversed. Since then there has been careful regulation of pollutants and many companies have been prosecuted under the Air Pollution and Water Pollution Control Laws. These laws have been amended several times and environmental pollution has generally been kept to a minimum.

Today there is official compensation for those who are victims of pollution. In 1981 there were 70,000 people who had been certified by the Environmental Agency as victims of pollution-related illnesses. The companies guilty of the pollution that affected such people have to pay compensation and medical expenses for as long as they are necessary.

Oil Shock and Trade Friction

In 1973 the Arab-Israeli war led to threats to cut off most of Japan's oil supplies and brought Arab demands for Japan to adopt an anti-Israel stance. At that time, Japan was dependent on oil for 70% of her energy needs, and 80% of this oil came from the Arab countries or Iran. Prices in the shops rose sharply as increasing oil costs were passed on to the consumer. For a few weeks there was panic buying of a wide range of goods, that even included toilet paper. As a result people began to lose confidence in large businesses which were already being criticised for pollution problems.

Japan was more vulnerable than any other major industrialised country to an increase in oil prices, or any restriction of oil supplies. The Arab-Israeli War caused rapid inflation and raised the price of Japanese exports. As a result, there was no trade surplus again until 1976. Despite this, Japan's economy survived the crisis and its industry demonstrated its strength and adaptability in the face of changing conditions.

The government tackled the problems of 1973 by encouraging energy saving and developing aid and trade with the Arab oil-producing countries. Since 1973 Japan has tried to diversify its supplies of oil and developed alternative sources of energy, such as nuclear power. Furthermore, by 1986 Japan required oil for only 60% of her energy needs.

The Iranian revolution of 1978-79 caused a second oil crisis. Drawing on the experiences of six years before, Japan managed to weather the crisis better than most industrialised nations. The production of electrical goods and cars, which required less energy began to be more important than the coal-and oil-thirsty steel and ship-building industries. High technology industries, such as microchip production, ceramics, fibre optics and lasers, which are all highly profitable, are now becoming more important than production of consumer goods.

Japanese stores sell cameras made in Indonesia, tape recorders from Korea and calculators from Hong Kong, as the manufacture of lower technology products is gradually moved to newly-industrialised countries with lower labour costs.

In recent years, the price of oil has fallen and Japan no longer has to achieve such massive exports to pay for supplies of raw materials, coal and oil. Furthermore, exports have increased dramatically, while imports have risen only slightly. This export surplus has been a source of friction with many of the countries that Japan has traded with since 1970. In that year there was trouble with the United States over unemployment in the American textile industry. Japanese manufacturers had to agree to limit textile sales to the United States when President Nixon imposed a 10% surcharge on imports.

Japan's huge domestic market has allowed strong industries to develop. These industries then used this base for massive exports. The problems of Japan's trade surplus have not just been because Japan has been exporting more than she imports. The imbalance has also been concentrated on specific types of goods, such as cars, TVs and video recorders. This has sometimes meant that European and American companies which were unable to compete, have been forced out of business. One example of this effect was the motor-cycle industry in Britain, which has almost ceased to exist in the face of imports of machines made by Honda, Yamaha, Suzuki, Kawasaki and other Japanese companies.

Tokyo's new international airport at Narita, Chiba prefecture; it opened in 1979 after years of delay, and is 60 kilometres from the city centre. What was the main cause of the delay?

In the face of western criticism MITI (the Ministry of International Trade and Industry) has fixed quotas of exports for some companies. Motor vehicle sales to the United States were fixed at just over 1.5 million for 1981, 1982 and 1983. Despite these restrictions the giant American company, General Motors has had to lay off many workers. Competition from Japanese imports was blamed for the company's problems.

Europeans have been similarly concerned about the imbalance of their trade with Japan. The French were drastic in their response, placing severe restrictions on the importing of TVs, videos, cars and motor-cycles. At the end of 1982 the French channelled all video recorder imports from Japan through one small customs post at Poitiers. This caused long delays, and supplies in French shops dried up almost completely. The measure was lifted after April 1983 when the Japanese agreed to limit further exports to France.

Restricting imports from Japan, or persuading the Japanese to agree to voluntary reductions in exports, has only been part of the problem. Western firms have also found it very difficult to sell their products in Japan. Some industries have been protected by tariffs, but these have been gradually dismantled under pressure from American and European governments. The strict safety standards for foreign products have also been relaxed since 1982. At the same time, inspection procedures for imported goods were simplified. These measures were designed to make it easier for western companies to export to Japan but Japan imports about a quarter less than she exports.

Some agricultural products are still protected, and the Americans have complained about the difficulty they have in selling beef, oranges and rice. The British have complained of unfair taxes affecting Britain's sales of whisky. In practice, variations in the exchange rate between the Japanese yen and other currencies has been more important in determining the price of imported goods in Japan than import tariffs. These have generally been less than 10%. The Japanese have also pointed to the fact that few European businessmen speak Japanese, as one of the reasons for the difficulties they experience in selling goods in Japan.

In 1986 exports to Europe increased by more than 50% in value. One reason for this was the increasingly angry reaction in the United States towards Japanese export successes. In the previous year 80% of Japan's trade surplus had been with America.

Japan has also managed to make important advances into the world money markets. Japanese banks have over 30% of international business in London while foreign banks have less than 3% of similar business in Tokyo.

Domestic Politics

From the early 1970s, to improve its popularity, government policies became more responsive to public opinion. Welfare and pollution control became important issues. Education provision improved and Japan now has one of the highest levels of literacy in the world and has almost two million students studying at universities. Education is such an important concern that the government has been prevented from imposing spending cuts because of public pressure. In the field of health care Japan is now a world leader with a greater number of hospital beds, proportional to the population, than any other country. Increasing pension and welfare benefits and money for regional development have meant that government spending has greatly exceeded its income since the early 1970s. Recent budgets have included large public expenditure cuts but despite this the deficit continues to grow.

The ruling Liberal Democratic Party (LDP) has managed to stay in power

Political Parties

LDP — The Liberal Democratic Party has by far the most seats in the Diet. From 1982-1987 it was led by Nakasone Yasuhiro who was also Prime Minister. Close relations with America are central to party policy. The LDP is a coalition of factions. The largest of these is the 'Tanaka' faction followed by those of Suzuki, Nakasone, Fukuda and Komoto. There are also a few party members who have seats in the Diet but do not belong to a particular faction.

JSP — The Japan Socialist Party was organised in November 1945. In 1951 the party split over the question of the peace treaty, but was reunited in 1955. There have been problems within the party over whether it should be one which represents a particular class or whether it should be a national party. The party has traditionally been anti-American and in favour of unarmed neutrality. These policies have been moderated in recent years.

KOMEITO — The Clean Government Party was founded in 1964 with the backing of Soka Gakkai a Buddhist group. Most of its support comes from the lower middle classes of the cities. The party is against any reform of the Constitution and in favour of greater independence from America.

DSP — The Democratic Socialist Party was launched in January 1960 from among former right-wing members of the Socialist Party. The party is anti-LDP and anti-communist but many of its policies are similar to those of the LDP.

JCP — The Japan Communist Party was founded in 1922 but collapsed under government repression before the last war. Since 1955 it has had a policy of peaceful revolution. In the elections of 1976 the party lost support and until 1986 it was the smallest of the opposition parties.

Under construction: one of many new bridges linking the numerous islands of the Seto Inland Sea with the main island of Honshu; this is the Shimotsui suspension bridge which has a centre span of 940 metres and is due to be completed in 1988

Polling station in a local school. What is the voting age in Japan?

since 1955 for three main reasons. It has demonstrated its continuing ability to govern. It has a proven record in achieving economic success, and the opposition has been divided. The party has become increasingly flexible in its policies as Japan has become more prosperous. The elections of 1977 left the LDP with a narrow majority in the Diet and it was forced to become more conscious of its public image. Most Japanese voters are unwilling to risk what they have by supporting parties that have no experience of holding office. None of the opposition parties has ever been strong enough to consider governing alone. In 1985 there were discussions by all the major opposition parties, except the communists, about forming coalitions. The main opposition group, the Japan Socialist Party (JSP) agreed in January 1986 to seek support from a broader section of the population and to consider a coalition with any other party. They did not even completely rule out working with the LDP itself in order to achieve some share in the government. The JSP also rejected eastern Euopean models of socialism while the more moderate, Democratic Socialist Party dropped the word 'socialism' from its programme altogether.

The LDP is a loose coalition of conservative factions that are prepared to work together to retain power. These factions have changed over the years, and conflict between them is sometimes fierce. All the factions have their own campaign headquarters and, as up to five members can represent each constituency, LDP candidates often find themselves competing against each other. The factions also influence the decisions that the Prime Minister has to make, including appointments to his cabinet which have to satisfy the different groups. Majorities do not tend to be particularly important in Japanese politics, and a consensus of agreement is more important. It is this factor which allows the government to function despite conflicts within the LDP itself.

Politicians are generally elected because of the connections that they, or their families, have within a constituency. The voters, particularly in rural areas, support candidates who can be relied upon to help their constituency in the Diet. It is usually important for a member to belong to one of the factions in order to increase the chances of government funds reaching the area he represents. The LDP gets much of its support from rural constituencies. The LDP can also be sure of support from owners of family businesses and shop-keepers, as there has been legislation to protect small shops from supermarket competition.

The 1986 Election

Over 70% of the 87 million registered voters turned out for the 1986 elections. In the House of Representatives the LDP increased its number of seats from 250 to 304. The Japan Socialist Party were reduced to 86 seats from 111. Komeito lost two of their 59 seats. The Democratic Socialists were cut from 37 to 26 seats. Only the Japan Communist Party did not lose any of its 27 seats to the LDP.

In the House of Councillors only half of the 252 seats were being fought for. The LDP gained twelve seats but there was little change in the representation of the other parties.

In recent years, voting in local elections has become more closely related to results in national contests. In April 1979 the LDP achieved significant gains at local level that included capturing control of the important governorships of Tokyo and Osaka. This was part of a general fall in support for left-wing parties.

After 1980 the LDP had an absolute majority in the Diet. Then the party lost 36 seats in the 1983 elections but retained its control of the Diet by inviting some independent members to join the party, and by forming a coalition with the New Liberal Club (NLC). The NLC decided to disband, and its members formally joined the LDP after its victory in the 1986 summer elections where it obtained a massive majority in both houses of the Diet. All other parties, except the communists, lost seats to the LDP, with the JSP and the Democratic Socialists being hardest hit.

The LDP now has to work out its response to a range of problems, all similar to those found in western countries. These include rising unemployment, reduction of large agricultural surpluses, public welfare spending, privatisation and educational reform.

The Lockheed Scandal

LDP rule has not been without incident. In 1974 the party president, Prime Minister Tanaka, resigned after criticism that he had gained some of his personal fortune through illegal methods.

Tanaka was the first post-war Prime Minister who did not receive a university education. He was the son of a farmer, and worked in a construction firm before forming his own company. He was elected to the Diet in 1947 and is thought to have spent enormous sums of money in his campaign to be elected to the

A typical urban street scene. What does this picture tell us about tradition and modern Japan?

leadership of the LDP. Because of the LDPs majority in the Diet this appointment carries with it the post of Prime Minister.

Tanaka was arrested in 1976 after investigations in America revealed that the Lockheed Corporation had been making payments to Japanese officials and politicians to try and gain contracts for civil and military aircraft. Tanaka was accused of using his influence to persuade All Nippon Airways to purchase the Lockheed Tristar. The prosecution claimed that he had been paid 500 million yen as a reward. Tanaka and his supporters have always maintained his innocence but he was fined and sentenced to four years imprisonment by the Tokyo district court. His lawyers appealed to the high court and he was released on bail. In July 1987 the Tokyo High Court upheld the original 1983 conviction but Tanaka's lawyers immediately appealed the ruling to the Supreme Court.

Tanaka resigned from the LDP and became an independent member of the Diet. His faction remained the largest in the party and he continued to be very influential. In the 1983 elections he received more votes than any other candidate. His constituency in central Japan is famous for getting a large share of government funds for regional development.

In February 1985 Tanaka entered hospital after a slight stroke and in June closed his political office. In summer 1987 his leadership of the faction was successfully challenged by the LDP's Secretary General, Takeshita Noboru which finally brought Tanaka's reign as 'king-maker' to an end. In October 1987 Takeshita himself was elected leader of the party and replaced Nakasone as Prime Minister the following month.

Defence

The Security Treaty with the United States was renewed with little opposition in 1970. Defence was no longer a major political issue in the early 1970s. In 1976 the government of Prime Minister Miki decided to limit expenditure on arms to a maximum of 1% of the GNP (Gross National Product). This figure remained the basis of policy until January 1987. The abandonment of this limit reflected American pressure for Japan to play a larger role in East-Asian defence. Together with trade, the defence issue has been a major problem in American-Japanese relations. In 1983 President Reagan visited Japan to discuss these questions. His visit helped ease tensions between the two countries, and he stressed American commitment to her treaty with Japan. Japanese public opinion is generally satisfied with the arrangements for defence based on American support.

Defence spending is about 1.5% of the GNP, if pensions for ex-servicemen and rents on land used by the armed forces are taken into account (as they are in all NATO estimates). Though there are a quarter of a million Japanese under arms this is fewer than in Korea or Taiwan, but Japan's air force is one of the best in Asia and in total, Japan's military expenditure is amongst the highest in the world.

Ships of Japan's Maritime Self-Defence Forces

The Japanese have rejected any idea of adopting nuclear weapons, though they certainly have the ability to produce them. Most Japanese see more prestige in being a nuclear-free power. Public opinion remains opposed to adopting nuclear weapons.

Since 1981, when Prime Minister Suzuki promised to defend the sea lanes around Japan, there has been an increasing commitment to defence by the Japanese government. Prime Minister Nakasone (elected in 1982) described Japan as a large aircraft carrier and plans for military development up to 1990 include greater emphasis on sea and air defences. In 1984 a military cooperation pact with the United States came into force and in April 1985 new American fighter bombers began to arrive for permanent station in Japan.

Japanese ships have taken part in joint naval exercises with America, Canada and Australia. The largest of these exercises occurred in October 1986 when

American and Japanese land sea and air forces conducted their first simultaneous combined operation. Five thousand men from each country and two hundred ships and aircraft were involved in a mock defence of Hokkaido.

Relations with Russia

Relations with Russia since 1970 have still been dominated by the failure to solve the problem of the Northern Territories — four small islands which Japan claims should be returned to her. In 1979 garrisons on the islands were increased and since then jet fighters have been stationed there. Russia has conducted extensive manoeuvres near the coasts of Japan and there have also been violations of Japanese air space by Russian military aircraft.

The Russian invasion of Afghanistan in 1979, the imposition of martial law in Poland in 1981 and the shooting down of the Korean airliner over Sakhalin in 1983 have all contributed to making Japan more disturbed by Soviet policy. Annual government defence reports have referred to the 'Soviet threat' since 1978. The Japanese have also been anxious about reported deployments of SS-20

HOKKAIDO & NORTHERN TERRITORIES

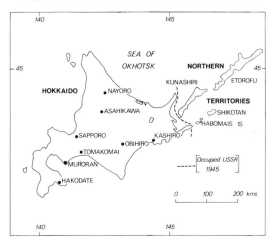

missiles in Asia, though the Russians have denied that these are specifically aimed at Japan.

Prime Minister Suzuki designated 7 February 'Northern Territories Day' and Prime Minister Nakasone said he was unwilling to visit the Soviet Union, or consider a formal peace, until the issue of the Northern Territories is resolved. Mr Gorbachev, the Russian leader, has rejected any change of status for the islands, but ex-residents have been allowed to visit the graves of their relatives — something which had not been allowed since 1976.

Despite their strained relations Japan has continued to trade with Russia, though trade levels have declined. By 1984 Japan had fallen from first to sixth place, in terms of the volume of trade between the Soviet Union and non-communist countries. Japan is also involved in several projects to develop Siberia,

The foreign ministers of Japan and China exchange copies of the 1978 Treaty of Peace and Friendship

including forestry, coal, and oil and gas exploration. Following the efforts of Mr Gorbachev to improve East-West relations, there have been agreements on fishing quotas, currency, transport and trade consultation.

Relations with China

In September 1972 Prime Minister Tanaka followed President Nixon's example and visited China. The American initiative had been without warning but the Japanese were quick to take advantage of the situation and open diplomatic relations with the People's Republic. In 1978 a formal treaty was signed and this effectively showed Japan's preference for China, rather than Russia.

Japan has been active in assisting with the modernisation of China and would like to improve its relations still further. Since the late 1970s trade has increased and Japan is now China's second largest trading partner. Japan has also provided loans and teaching programmes to speed the growth of China's economy. One problem is China's increasing inability to balance her trade with Japan. Japan has received some oil but Chinese oil has only provided a few per cent of Japan's imports in any one year.

The imbalance in trade is now a serious problem in relations between Japan and China, though both countries are keen that it should have no lasting effect. The trade deficit for 1985 was $6 billion and for 1986, $4 billion. There has been some increase in Japanese investment in China over recent years but the Chinese would like more. They also want the Japanese to buy more of their goods and increase loans.

Japan's World Role

In recent years, the Japanese have become increasingly conscious of their important place in world affairs. Prime Minister Nakasone said that this role should be equal to Japan's economic importance.

Japan is second only to the United States in its contributions to the budget of the United Nations and in its overseas aid. Japan also has a good record of

The new face of Tokyo: 'Ark Hills', completed in 1986, includes a 37-storey 'intelligent' office building, a hotel, a condominium, a concert hall and a television studio

practical industrial training for the Third World. At least 50,000 people from developing countries arrive in Japan each year to study technical and industrial skills. Japan's Overseas Cooperation Volunteers have been successful in working in Third World countries as teachers and in local development projects.

Vietnam's invasion of Cambodia and Vietnam's pro-Russian alignment, have made the countries in South-East Asia look to Japan for support against communist expansion. Japan has strengthened its relations with ASEAN (The Association of South-East Asian Nations) since its formation in 1967. In 1976 a treaty of friendship and trade was signed with Australia and the two countries are now important trading partners.

Japan is now one of the most influential countries in the Pacific area and is taking an increasingly prominent part in world politics. Japan participates in the Summit meetings of the advanced industrialised countries and has become, with Western Europe and the USA, one of the three most important pillars of the non-communist world.

Leaders of the seven Summit countries and the European Community at the Tokyo Summit, May 1986. From left to right: EC Commission President Jacques Delors, Bettino Craxi (Italy), Dutch Prime Minister Rudolphus Lubbers (as EC Council Chairman), Helmut Kohl (West Germany), Ronald Reagan (USA), Nakasone Yasuhiro (Japan), Francois Mitterand (France), Margaret Thatcher (Great Britain) and Brian Mulroney (Canada)

POINTS TO CONSIDER

1.   In the 1970s the government turned its attentions increasingly towards improving the living conditions of the Japanese people.
2.   The 'oil shock' of 1973 brought about a change in industrial development, and a realisation that Japan needed good relations with a wider range of countries.
3.   The LDP has remained in power because it has responded to public opinion and has been flexible in its policies. Lack of opposition unity has also been an important factor.
4.   Relations with China have improved while those with Russia have remained generally cool.
5.   Japan's export successes have led to difficulties in her relations with several trading partners.
6.   The government has become increasingly confident in dealing with Japan's problems as the nation emerges as an influential world power.

QUESTIONS

(a)   How successfully has Japan dealt with its recent problems in foreign relations?
(b)   Describe domestic politics in Japan since 1970.

Glossaries

CHAPTER 1

SHOGUN AND MEIJI

Blockade: preventing supplies moving by sea in an attempt to force the enemy to give in.

Daimyo: a lord in charge of a feudal domain or province.

Diet: Japan's 'parliament' made up of two Houses, Peers and Representatives, of roughly equal powers.

Constitution: the document providing the basic rules for governing the country.

House of Representatives: the Lower House of the Diet with 300 members who were first elected in 1890 by a small section of the male population.

Marquis: a noble ranking below a prince. All marquises over 25 were members of the House of Peers.

Nationalism: loyalty and devotion to and pride in one's own country.

Opium War: war fought between Britain and China from 1840-42 partly over the trade in opium. Britain gained Hong Kong in the treaty settlement that followed the war.

Samurai: a member of the warrior class who was allowed to carry two swords.

Triple Intervention: when the three powers, Russia, France and Germany, demanded that Japan return the Liaotung Peninsula to China after the end of Sino-Japanese war in 1895.

CHAPTER 2

MODERNISATION

Censorship: control of books, newspapers and the media to prevent publication of ideas opposed to those of the government.

Centralised system: political system in which central government has wide powers and control.

National Assembly: parliament.

Slander and libel laws: laws to control an individual's right to criticise another, either by word or in writing.

The West: the economically-developed countries of Western Europe and North America.

CHAPTER 3

TAISHO DEMOCRACY

Bolshevik: Russian communist supporters of Lenin.

Bureaucracy: government officials.

Elder Statesman: an old experienced politician whose advice was often sought.

Genro: an unofficial group of senior statesmen acting as advisers to the emperor and helping to choose Prime Ministers.

House of Peers: the Upper House in the Diet, under the Meiji Constitution, composed of members of the Emperor's family, nobles and some of the highest taxpayers.

Intellectuals: intelligent and well educated people, often professors, writers or artists.

Minseito: political party formed in 1927; dependent on support from townspeople and business interests.

Seiyukai: formed by Ito Hirobumi in 1900; most of its support came from the countryside.

Socialists: those who believed in control of industry by the government or the workers themselves.

Zaibatsu: (literally 'financial clique') a group of companies (conglomerate) that dominated Japan's economy up to 1945 and were often controlled by one family, such as Mitsui and Mitsubishi.

CHAPTER 4

EARLY INDUSTRY

Deflationary policy: policy aimed to control price levels and to reduce government spending.

Industrialisation: the process of developing modern industries, such as shipbuilding, iron and steel, and modern armaments.

Inflation: an increase in the level of prices.

Investment: money used to buy new machinery, develop new products and expand production in industry.

Productivity: quantity of goods produced per worker, factory or industry.

Raw materials: basic items essential for the modern industries, such as iron ore and coal.

Subsidies: government grants of money to help the development and expansion of industry.

CHAPTER 5

THE THIRTIES

Demilitarised Zone: area where no armed forces are allowed.

Comintern: short for Communist International, set up in 1919 to spread communist ideas around the world.

Expansionist Policy: plans to take over other areas and countries.

Kodo: The Imperial Way faction in the army regarded Russia as Japan's main enemy.

League of Nations: an organisation founded in 1920 to try to keep world peace.

Nazi Germany: Germany (after 1933) under the rule of Hitler's Nazi party.

Tariffs: tax levied by government on imports.

Tenant Farmers: farmers who rented the land they worked.

Tosei: Control faction in the army, interested in expansion in China.

CHAPTER 6

EDUCATION

Absenteeism: failure of pupils to attend school.

Calligraphy: writing of Chinese characters and Japanese syllables with a brush.

Confucius (adjective — Confucian): a Chinese philospher (551-479 BC) who believed in the importance of loyalty, respect, honesty, humanity, education etc.

Curriculum: subjects studied in school.

Ethics: correct attitudes and behaviour.

Martial arts: methods of self-defence, e.g. karate.

Rescript: a command from the Emperor.

Urbanisation: growth of towns and cities.

CHAPTER 7

JAPAN AT WAR

Alliance: military agreement between countries.

Black-market: goods bought and sold illegally.

Guerilla: irregular soldier.

Incendiary: bomb designed to start fires.

Intelligence: military information about an enemy's armed forces.

Nationalism: loyalty or devotion to one's own country.

Neutrality Agreement: agreement between countries not to fight if the other becomes involved in a war.

Non-Aggression Pact: agreement between two countries not to fight each other.

Unconditional Surrender: giving in completely to an enemy.

CHAPTER 8

COUNTRYSIDE

Arbitration: system for settling disputes.

Brazier: metal container for burning hot coals.

Carbohydrates: foods such as rice and barley which satisfy hunger but have limited nutritional value.

Irrigation: watering of fields using water channels.

Landlord: man with tenants living or working on his land and paying some form of rent.

Mechanisation: introduction of mechanical aids to farming, e.g., tractors.

Reclamation: filling in of coastal land for farming.

Tax in kind: payment of taxes by goods (e.g., rice) instead of money.

World depression: collapse of the world economy in the late 1920s.

CHAPTER 9

OCCUPATION

Benevolent: showing good will, friendly.

Constitution: the document detailing the way that a country is governed.

Decentralise: reorganise and disperse into smaller units.

Democracy: government by the people's elected representatives.

Diet: Japan's 'parliament' made up of two Houses, Councillors and Representatives.

Kamikaze: popular name used for Japan's special suicide-attack squads.

Prefecture: one of 47 districts, similar to an English county, each with its own governor.

SCAP: Supreme Commander for the Allied Powers, title given to General Douglas MacArthur during the Occupation.

Tuberculosis: disease caused by infection, usually in the lungs, sometimes called consumption.

CHAPTER 10

WOMEN

Conservative: preferring established ways of doing things, cautious about change, and respecting order and authority.

Liberal ideas: ideas that emphasise, the freedom and rights of the individual.

Munitions: military equipment.

Redundant: the loss of one's job due to company reorganisation, financial problems.

Suffrage Bill: the bill of 1925 that gave males over 25 the right to vote.

CHAPTER 11
GROWING PROSPERITY
Commission: groups set up by the government with particular powers to investigate something.

Constitution: the document detailing the way that a country is governed.

Indoctrination: enforced acceptance of ideas.

Okinawa: largest of the Ryuku group of islands situated south-west of Kyushu.

Prefecture: one of 47 districts, similar to an English county, each with its own governor.

Rearmament: rebuilding and equipping the armed forces.

Reparations: compensation a defeated country pays to another to make amends.

Security Pact: agreement between countries on defence measures in case of war.

CHAPTER 12
POST-WAR INDUSTRY
Capital-intensive industries: industries which require expensive plant and machinery, such as shipbuilding and steel.

Communications: road and rail systems, telephone and postal services.

Components: parts used in manufacturing, e.g., mirrors for cars.

Dissolution: the breaking up of the *zaibatsu* into smaller business units.

Enterprises: businesses.

Investment capital: money used to help industry grow, and to provide new plant and machinery.

Korean War: conflict between communist North Korea assisted by China and non-communist South Korea assisted by United Nations forces, including the USA and Britain. The war lasted from 1950 to 1953.

Oil Shocks: the dramatic rises in the price of Middle East oil which took place in 1973 and 1978.

Purge: removal from office of those who worked closely with military dominated governments of 1932-45.

Respiratory diseases: diseases connected with breathing, such as asthma, emphysema etc.

Tariff wall: control of foreign imports by system of high customs duties.

CHAPTER 13
JAPAN TODAY
Cadmium: bluish-white metallic element used in electroplating and alloys.

Coalition: a temporary alliance between groups or parties.

Consensus: general agreement, collective opinion.

Deployment: prepare troops or weapons ready for battle.

Disunity: become separate because of disagreements.

Diversify: produce a greater variety of products to reduce risk.

Environment: the surroundings and conditions in which people live and work.

Quotas: enforced limit on a number or quantity of a type of product which can be imported or exported.

Surcharge: an extra charge, such as a tax, on top of the usual payment.

Trade deficit: when the amount imported is more than that exported.

TRADITION AND MODERN JAPAN

Tradition and modern Japan: (above) traditional tea ceremony which first came from China in the fifteenth century; (below) individual uranium rods being loaded into an atomic pile by a precise crane. What connections could be made between these two pictures? What do they say about Japan today?

SUGGESTIONS FOR FURTHER READING

Of the standard histories of modern Japan teachers will find the following most useful:

W. G. Beasley *The Modern History of Japan.* 3rd edition. Weidenfeld, 1981.
Richard Storry *The History of Modern Japan.* Penguin, 1969. (minor revisions in later printings)

A very thorough and scholarly overview of the full range of Japanese history can be found in:

Edwin O. Reischauer and **Albert M. Craig** *Japan: Tradition and transformation.* Allen & Unwin, 1979.

A good survey of post-war Japan is provided by:

Roger Buckley *Japan Today.* Cambridge UP, 1985.
Peter Duus *The Rise of Modern Japan.* Houghton Mifflin, 1976
Kenneth B. Pyle *The making of Modern Japan.* D. C. Heath, 1978.
John Whitney *Japan from Pre-History to Modern Times.* Dell Publishing and Weidenfeld & Nicholson, 1970.

A very useful guide full of teaching and reading suggestions is:

Richard Tames *The Japan Handbook: a Guide for Teachers.* 2nd edition. Paul Norbury Publications, 1981

SOURCES FOR DOCUMENTS

CH 2: MODERNISATION

2. **Chamberlain,** *Things Japanese,* 3rd revised edition. London: Murray, 1898, 7-8.
3. **Fukuzawa Yukichi,** *Autobiography,* translated by Eiichi Kiyooka. New York: Columbia UP, 1966, 246-247.
4. **Yazaki Takeo** Social change and the city, cited in The Japan reader, edited, annotated and with introductions by Jon Livingston, Joe Moore and Felicia Oldfather. Volume One: *Imperial Japan 1800-1945.* Harmondsworth: Penguin, 1976, 135-6.
5. **Okuma Shigenobu,** cited in *Sources of Japanese Tradition,* op. cit., 187.

CH 4: EARLY INDUSTRY

1. **Hane Mikiso** *Peasants, rebels and outcastes: the underside of modern Japan.* New York: Pantheon, 1982, 196.
2. ibid, 189.
3. **Basil Hall Chamberlain,** op. cit., 220-1.
4. **Hane** op cit., 182.

CH 6: EDUCATION

1. **Herbert Passin** *Society and education in Japan.* Tokyo: Kodansha, 1982, 212-3.
2. **Isabella Bird,** *Unbeaten tracks in Japan .* London: Virago, 1984, 71-2 (originally published by Murray, 1880)
3. **John Morris,** *Traveller from Tokyo.* London: Cresset Press/Readers' Union, 1944, 34-41 (originally published 1943)
4. **Passin,** op. cit., 301-2.
5. National Council on Educational Reform (Government of Japan) Second report on educational reform, April 1986.

CH 8: COUNTRYSIDE

1. **Hane,** op. cit., 62-3.
2. **J. W. Robertson Scott** *The foundations of Japan.* New York: Appleton, 1922, cited in The Japan Reader, volume 1, edited by Jon Livingston, Joe Moore and Felicia Oldfather. Harmondsworth: Penguin, 1976, 29-30.
3. **Smith** and **Wiswell,** op. cit., xxix.
4. **Ronald Dore,** *Shinohata: a portrait of a Japanese village.* London: Allen Lane, 1978, 104-5.
5. Ministry of Agriculture, Forestry and Fisheries. Annual report on agriculture, 1983 (April 1984).

CH 10: WOMEN

1. **Chamberlain,** op. cit., 424-5.
2. *Sources of Japanese tradition,* volume 2, compiled by Tsunoda Ryusaku, W.T. de Bary and Donald Keene. New York: Columbia UP, 1958, 274-5.
3. **Robert J. Smith** and **Ella Lury Wiswell** *The women of Suye Mura* London: Chicago UP, 1982, xxxvii.
4. **Tsurumi Kazuko** *Social change and the individual: Japan before and after defeat in World War II.* Princeton (NJ): Princeton UP, 1970, 297-8.
5. **James Trager** (ed) *Letters from Sachiko: a Japanese woman's view of life in the land of the economic miracle.* London: Sphere (Abacus), 1984, 28.

CH 12: POST-WAR INDUSTRY

1. Cited in **Richard T. Pascale** and **Anthony G. Athos** *The art of Japanese management.* Penguin, 1982.
2. Cited in **Ronald Dore** *British factory — Japanese factory: the origins of national diversity in industrial relations.* Allen & Unwin, 1973, 164.
3. **Tanaka Kakuei** *Building a new Japan: a plan for remodelling the Japanese archipelago.* Tokyo: Simul Press, 1973, 77-8.
4. 'Clash of the titans,' Economist 23-29 August 1986.
5. **Dick Wilson** *The sun at noon: an anatomy of modern Japan.* Hamish Hamilton, 1986, 153-154.

Acknowledgements

ILLUSTRATIONS PAGE REFERENCES

Asahi Shimbun 94, 95
Beato, Felix XII, 14
British Museum 3
Brownell, Clarence 101
Dore, R.P. 87
Greenlees, John 136, 143
Hideo Aoki 47
Illustrated London News 43
International Society for Ecucational Information
      (ISEI) X, 1, 5, 8, 45, 53, 55, 67, 88, 90, 104,
      107, 117, 120, 126, 129, 141, 147
Japan Information Centre 12, 99, 64
Japan Library Ltd 75, 131, 140
Japan Pictorial 15, 60, 108
Keystone Press 63
Kyodo 93
Mary Evans Picture Library 30
Ministry of Foreign Affairs (Japan) 37, 50, 56, 60,
      71, 74, 99, 115, 122, 144, 146, 148
Pedlar, Neil 10
Prime Minister's Office (Japan) 133, 134, 155
Shogakukan, Tokyo 6, 10, 64, 69
Smith, Howard 89
Smith, R.J. 84
Tsuneo Tamba 21
Tokyo National Museum 4
Tokyo Shoseki Publishing Co 146
US Navy 68, 192
US Army 74

Every effort has been made to contact the copyright
holders of the illustrations published in this book;
where it has not been possible to do so, the publishers
apologise for any inconvenience caused.

TEXTS PAGE REFERENCES

A full list of sources for the documents quoted in this
book are published on page 156ff; every effort has
been made to contact the copyright holders; where it
has not been possible to do so, the publishers
apologise for any inconvenience caused.

TABLES PAGE REFERENCES

Enrolment rate in compulsory education 51
(International Society for Educational Information)

Japan's School System 59
(Ministry of Education, Science & Culture)

*Relative positions of Gross National Products of Selected
Countries (1951-1982)* 116
(Bank of Japan, Keizai Koho Center)

Growth trends of real Per Capita GNP (1880-1980)
127
(Paul A. Samuelson, 'Economics' 11th Edn,
McGraw-Hill/Keizai Koho Center)

Index

NOTE: *Numbers in bold refer to picture captions*